The Voice of One Crying In the Wilderness

God's Marvelous Light Healed Me

By Princess, Prophetess Dr. Sasha Lecher, PhD.

A Spiritual, Inspirational Autobiography

"Severe Darkness"

The Voice of One Crying In The Wilderness
Copyright © 2015 by **Dr. Sasha Lecher, PhD.**
All rights reserved.

No part of this publication may be reproduced, stored in a retrieval system or transmitted in any way by any means, electronic, mechanical, photocopy, recording or otherwise, without the prior permission of the author except as provided by USA copyright law.

All characters appearing in this work are fictitious. Any resemblance to real persons, living or dead is purely coincidental.

The opinions expressed by the author are not necessarily those of Revival Waves of Glory Books & Publishing.

Published by Revival Waves of Glory Books & Publishing
PO Box 596| Litchfield, Illinois 62056 USA
www.revivalwavesofgloryministries.com

Revival Waves of Glory Books & Publishing is committed to excellence in the publishing industry.

Book design copyright © 2015 by Revival Waves of Glory Books & Publishing. All rights reserved.

Paperback: 978-1-68411-218-0

Published in the United States of America

FOREWORD

My mother, Princess, Prophetess Dr. Sasha Lecher had a hard struggle all her life and she learned God is the only answer when you're in darkness. To be rejected and cast out from everyone you love is a traumatic loss of a social life that once was a source of fulfillment.

Being in darkness is a terrible opposition that one has to face on their own. Being weak does not make you less of a human being. Prophetess Sasha hid in silence for many years and escaped through many vanities. Jesus said, "MY GRACE IS SUFFICIENT FOR YOU, FOR MY POWER IS MADE PERFECT IN WEAKNESS". (2 COR. 12:9)

By Princess Evangelist Corinthia Ariella Yocheved

Table of Contents

FOREWORD 4

INTRODUCTION 7

ACKNOWLEDGEMENTS 8

Chapter One A Prophetess Is Born 10

Chapter Two Mama's Little Blessings 16

Chapter Three Family Chaos 23

Chapter Four Discovering My Youth 30

Chapter Five Isolation Days 51

Chapter Six Being Born Again 65

Chapter Seven Driven in the wilderness 80

Chapter Eight (The Apple of His EYE) The Covenant Restored 105

Autobiography 112

INTRODUCTION

Living my life as a female became one of my hardest struggles and one of my deepest pains. I went through a period of finding God and then losing God, being stripped of all my spiritual blessings and earthly blessings.

All my life I have been abused and suffered many losses; one of them was so devastating to my entire well-being, the temporary loss of my twelve-year daughter in May of 2002.

To have your only child illegally kidnapped and tortured for three years made me analyze my position with God, and I asked the question, "Why did God change on me?" Why did he become so cold? How could I find his favor again?

ACKNOWLEDGEMENTS

I like to honor first my awesome, omniscient, spiritual father, Jehovah God, and my beautiful Lord and Savior whom is also my true and only friend, Jesus Christ.

The Lord has been the main instrument that has held me together. He is the strength and the wisdom that helped me complete this book.

He is the calm hand that I felt touch me through days of distress, and He is the warm spirit that has embraced me and given me peace.

Second, I like to give thanks to my only and special beloved daughter whom was a great inspiration to me throughout my life.

My daughter, Princess Corinthia Ariella Yocheved, was the reality of my life, whom the Lord blessed me to have as a friend to love and to share good times with.

Through our darkness, we cried together and we recovered together. We're a great mom and daughter team. I owe this book all to you. (My beloved daughter)

(Love, your mom and friend)

I like to thank my mom, Princess Dr. Janice Yancey/Yocheved Ph.D. Biblical Studies who bore me and showed me the first five years of life. My mom taught me the importance and the reverence of our Lord Jesus Christ.

That everything is through him and by him. My mom laid it down early to me that Jesus is the creator and I am the creature. I must acknowledge and give thanks and worship him in all. Amen.

I like to give thanks to the Lord. It would not have happened if it would not have been for him giving me the opportunity to publicly become known as a prophet on television.

I thank them greatly.

I will like to show my utmost gratitude to "TBN America and Israel" and I also thank the Lord for your existence and creative mind to expose the Gospel of peace to a dying and lost nation. Amen.

I like to give my thanks to "Revival Waves of Glory Publishing" Create Space, Charisma Media, Tate Christian and Dorrance Publishing for their committed work and belief in my talent. If it was not for them, I would not have the opportunity to share with the world my challenging testimony. I thank you all. May the Lord bless you to continue to grow and help others.

My brother, Prince Dwayne Yancey/Yocheved, Evangelist B.A. Divinity... I thank him for his loyalty and integrity. He stood up for me when I needed a stronger hand. He was the voice that corrected many of my foes that were too big for me. I thank Dwayne for being a dedicated baby brother. I pray blessings on his life and that he will become a minister of God.

Chapter One
A Prophetess Is Born

Nine thirty in the morning, a Princess of the House of Joseph (Israel), and Prophetess was born. "Royalty's" parent's Victor and Janice Yancey had a healthy seven pound, eight ounce female named Latosha Marie Yancey...a full blood Hebrew, Creole full blood Cherokee Indian with British ancestry.

My parents were a very odd match. My mother, Princess Janice practiced Jehovah's Witness, and my dad practiced nothing. My mom was born in Pontiac, Michigan, a satisfying (Upper Middle Class) suburban place to live with her parents and grandparents.

Mama was born to James Simmons, a young, handsome nineteen-year-old British, Cherokee Creole American army soldier. James had humble, graceful, beautiful beginnings, being born to a British, Creole, American father, William, who also served honestly in the United States as a farmer.

His mother, Ella, was a devoted Jehovah's Witness. She was very beautiful and was raised in Sumter, Alabama. She was of British, Irish, and French descent and full blood Cherokee Indian.

Ella's father was British; a mixture of European blends such as French and Irish. He was considered a wealthy Barrister with a Christian background. Ella's mother was also of the Christian religion.

She inherited a conservative upbringing through her mother's devoted Baptist order.

Ella's mother, Janet, was a tall, beautiful woman who was made with a beautiful blend of Cherokee Indian and that makes her full blooded Indian.

I consider myself a beautiful blend of British, Creole American, Irish, French, Indian, and Hebrew Israelite - A Seminole Princess of Israel. My appearance expresses all these unique blends: the fair and golden-sun complexion, the hazel dove shaped brown eyes; exquisite high cheek bones, and long synthetic dark black hair. My skin burns in the summer to a red pottage Morocco color. I inherited my mother's 5'7" height. We both are very beautiful people and devoted to religion. I have a passive, meek, and quiet spirit that came only from mother.

My mother's mom, Flossie Dickerson, (my grandmother) was born in Montgomery, Alabama. A full blood Indian, Alaskan... Flossie was of a Baptist background. She was the youngest of all her siblings. My grandmother was a very pretty young lady, who resembled Eartha Kitt. She was a petite lady with class, dignity, and loyalty to her family.

At seventeen, she met my granddad in Montgomery, Alabama, while serving in the army. They married right away and she left her family and headed up north to Pontiac. Ms. Flossie bore thirteen children. She had two single children, one set of triplets, and four sets of twins. My mom was the second, single eldest daughter. Our family make-up was, I can say, huge.

My father, Victor Yancey, has faith in God. Both of his parents believe in God. His parentage started in Milwaukee, Wisconsin. He was born in 1956. His mom was a full blood Creole Indian with British Creole heritage.

His father was an intelligent full blood "Creole American Native" who was very witty, outspoken, and a careful man. He laid down things that needed to be laid down.

Mr. Senior Yancey met his beautiful wife, Dede, a full blood Indian with British and Hebrew Israelite ancestry; tribe of Joseph descendant when they were young.

They had a very long relationship that consisted of many children. Richard, Alonzo, Timothy, Doreen, Hattie and a few others. My father, Victor, was the baby boy; he was spoiled and didn't get along with most of his siblings.

Mr. Victor Yancey was a British Creole full blooded Indian, 100%...

When my dad was an adolescent, he hung around his eldest brother Alonzo. He was the most peculiar man I have ever laid eyes on as a child. He had beautiful British blonde features and he just stood out among the rest. We called him Fuzzy. However, he was a natural blonde with blue eyes...My dad and Uncle Fuzzy began a nice, long-term relationship.

My dad met my mom at North Division High School. Mr. Victor Yancey was seventeen years old and Princess Ms. Janice Yancey was sixteen years old. They fell in love for all eternity.

Victor was attracted to my mom's shyness and her love of reading books. When he passed by her in the high school hallways, she would be reading a book, and Victor would just walk up to her and embrace her with a hug, and say, "Miss Yancey, may I read this book with you?"

They were a unique couple. On the other hand, Janice was drawn by Victor's masculinity and his love for wrestling, and yet he was a sentimental person. They started their moonlight and candles a little early. At seventeen, my mom was pregnant and her family went nuts.

Janice's mom was not very fond of my father. They felt he was sort of too weird. For instance, he would sleep over with Janice. Of course, he wasn't allowed to sleep in the same room with her, but instead of sleeping on the couch, he would be found in the basement, sleeping only to the sound of the washing machine.

He was so crazy for them. I remember my grandmother saying when I lived with her as a teenager that my father was a fool. Maybe he was but yet I still had some respect for him, even when all others had not.

Furthermore, mom was a Jehovah's Witness, so becoming pregnant caught her by surprise. She wanted to do the right thing, so marriage was the first thing that came to her mind. Before she mentioned marriage to Victor, he asked her to marry him. Janice said, "Yes," and she asked that Jehovah forgive her sins of fornication and be pleased to honor her marriage.

However, they didn't marry until after I was born, because she had not reached eighteen years of age yet. Therefore, they married six months prior to their second child being born.

Everyone in the Simmons family was excited to embrace the first daughter, grandchild, and niece. My grandmother was given the honor to name me. She picked an American girl's name, Latosha, and gave me her middle name Marie. I was Latosha Marie Yancey, and I was a beautiful child.

My first year of life was surrounded by extended family members. My grandmother's house which was a brick single family home on Monroe Street consisted of most of her kids, even though some had their own homes.

My mom and dad shared a cozy upper duplex not far from downtown Milwaukee. Everyone loved having me over. My mom's baby sister and baby brother would always come in and pick me up from our two family duplex.

My aunt, Michelle, being an adolescent would ride her bike over from Monroe Street, which was located on the west side of Milwaukee, just to visit me. Michelle was a fraternal twin, her soul brother was Michael, a future Navy officer turned religious leader.

On one sunny afternoon, my mom took me to have pictures with Peterman. It was a nice bonding engagement. My mom took me to several nice outings on many occasions that were not very expensive.

My mother continued her Jehovah studies, and my father attended most of them with her because of his love for her. My mom didn't take on any job; her religion's doctrine was that the husband was to be the sole provider.

My dad was employed at a small factory. It was all he could find at eighteen and having a high school diploma so he only had a limited moderate income.

Janice received much help with raising me. Her two sisters, Karen and Christine Simmons, pitched in a lot with my care. Karen was the third eldest sister, a triplet; however, her two soul sisters died at birth. Karen helps my mom a lot and she bought many gifts over to the house.

I love the family bond on my mother's side. Christine, the fourth sibling, also a fraternal twin, and her soul brother, Christopher, was born on New Year's. Christine was more like my mother; shy and mysterious. I was surrounded by love of many and deeply appreciated. However, what they didn't know I was born to be a special prophet of the Lord.

Chapter Two
Mama's Little Blessings

The first five years of life were all about being nurtured and learning baby basics and remembering my family member's faces.

A baby boy was born, a second of five talented children. Victor Yancey, Jr. was born July 14, 1976. The home was no longer occupied with just me. I had a special friend to run around the house with.

Father continued to work and supplied our needs. Meanwhile, mom prepared the meals and taught us the meaning of giving thanks to Jehovah God in his beloved son Jesus Christ name. That prayer was our daily devotion prior to our meals and at night a prayer of protection.

Victor and I would run through the house and we would play hide-go-seek. We were three and four-year-olds living it up.

On the other hand, Mom was pregnant again with her third child. She was a beautiful, healthy, eight-pound baby girl. Princess Lisa Renee Yancey was the third oldest, who grew up to be an independent liberalist, and confidante and also whom broke my heart.

Being the eldest, I was the first kid to start school. I was very excited to begin kindergarten class and asked mom all sorts of questions. I attended a suburban school called South 88 Street School. Mother bought me about four school outfits, school supplies, and a book bag to begin class.

I was a little timid once school actually started. However, I remember after the first day of class, I was all warmed up and could not wait to attend again.

The following year, I was enrolled in another suburban elementary school, South Seventy Eight Street School. My brother, Prince Victor, attended my second year with me.

One day, my aunt Michelle picked me up from my parent's house and took me to grandma's house. Everyone was over, because grandma got sick and had to go to the hospital. Karen and Christine were left out with their kids.

Meanwhile, I was led to go out to the backyard while it was yet very dark. All of a sudden, grandma's dog came near to me, growling with red eyes. I was terrified and ran up the steps to the front porch and went to the door and it was locked and the dog was coming towards me very fast. I was panicking and screaming, "Open the door, Aunt Michelle!" She was on the phone and told me to hush up so I ran across the street towards my aunt's as they were getting into the car. The next thing I saw was a huge light and I blacked out. I had been hit by a car.

My grandmother told me years later how my car accident took place and how everyone was startled. Aunt Karen was hollering. My aunt Christine was going mad and yelling. She kept fainting and going in and out. The paramedics had to sustain her and was about to put her in the ambulance with me. I blanked out all the way to the hospital.

As I arrived at the hospital, they began immediate surgery. My mom told me I was out for at least fifteen hours and was heavily sedated. I nearly awakened to see surgeons operating on me, but I was still heavily sedated. I had one leg hanging up with a metal pin going through one side of my leg to the other. I felt some needle pain, however, I was back to sleep.

The following morning, I received visits from my family members including momma, dad, Aunt Michelle, and Aunt Christine. But being hospitalized was awful. I had to suffer and go through a routine of medical procedures requiring daily drawing of blood, urine, x-rays, and some days, minor surgery. I believe I spent about two weeks in the hospital. I had to wear a full body cast which became a stressor to mom.

I was glad to be departing from the hospital. Little did I know, my family had moved into a two bedroom apartment not far from our previous residence. Mom had to carry me up a flight of steps of our new apartment. I asked mom why we had to move. She said because the rent was cheaper and we were on the waiting list for a three bedroom townhouse, with two baths. The apartments were called McKinley Gardens and they were located on the west side of Milwaukee. That was soon to be our residence for the next five years. However, one of my darkest moments occurred there, besides my accident.

Mama's little girl, her firstborn daughter, had to recover from a serious car accident. During my recovery period, there was only one person I gave my blessings to, the one and only parent that I am close to. Oh, how I loved my mother; she was very warm to me. She nursed me well.

My father was detached from me and he had a lot of stress on his shoulders. I guess he was agitated, because when I asked him one question, he yelled at me to go to sleep. He didn't care that I was in a cast and had just gotten out the hospital. I guess, being a man, that's the way he handled his hurt.

I, Latosha, felt like a burden to both of my parents because of the accident. Having to wear a full body cast was a bit stressful to them, especially mom. Meanwhile, all I could do was wait until my cast was removed. I watched my younger sisters and brothers' play around my bed. I wished I was able to run and play with them. I missed going to school! I felt lonely and sorrowful.

As I laid in silence, I felt something warm. It was a nice spirit all around me and I was comforted by it. I sensed it was God. This was the first phenomena of more to come that I experienced. I was so young but yet I believed it was the living God watching over me.

Monday morning was very dull. My dad awakened me, yelling at my mom about Lisa crying excessively. She was the baby girl and required a lot of attention. Mom quieted her down and went in the kitchen to make breakfast.

Victor was asleep in the upper bunk. I slept in the lower bunk. The room we shared was plain. We had a five-drawer chest and some animated curtains, a couple of toys and one small plastic table with two chairs. I wished that I had a TV in my room, verses being placed in the living room on the couch to watch TV.

Mom didn't allow us to watch certain programs because of our religion, and a lot of things were cancelled out such as birthdays and holidays. I was upset about both. My grandma was a Baptist Christian so she celebrated birthdays and Christmas. I was able to enjoy those celebrated moments in her home.

Finally, I had a doctor appointment and cast removal for Miss Latosha Yancey came. Hallelujah, thank you Jesus. That was a blessed day. The doctor just said it would take a couple more weeks before I got adjusted to walking again so I had to use crutches. I went out healthy and strong.

In three weeks, we were to move into the three bedroom townhouse. I missed having a normal childhood, and being able to run around. I had to continue resting and spending long periods by myself. I would just lie in bed looking at Sears's magazines, wishing we were richer. I wanted a full house!

I was also a dreamer. I dreamed all sorts of things. One of my weirdest dreams was swimming in a lake showered with lots of children swimming in and out of it and there was a huge rainbow over us. This dream was very soothing to me and gave me peace and tranquility when I had pain from my car accident. I believe it was Jesus showing his love for me.

One evening, mom sat all the children down to read the book of Bible stories. I lay on the small couch. It was very difficult for me to sit up. However, I loved when mom gave us Bible studies. Commenting on the questions of the Bible was my favorite subject. Mama would read from the story of Daniel in the lion's den. It is a story of courage and believing God when in danger.

Life as a little five-year old couldn't be better. One day, I had a great desire to just binge on chocolate ice cream. I begged my mother to go out and buy ice cream. She was very nice and took my brother, Victor, to Sentry's grocery store when my father got home. Being a recovered car accident victim got me a lot of special attention.

After one week and a half, I fully recovered and walked very well. The crutches were out of my life. I was a normal kid again. It was February, 1981 and we had a new entertainment center and select TV, which was an alternative to cable television.

My father received a settlement from my car accident and bought a large floor model color television and a brand new Sanyo stereo system. With her share of it, Mom bought a set of new chairs for the kitchen, large paintings for the living room and new bedding for all of our bedrooms.

The lawyer in charge of our settlement closed some of the amount and left a nice chomp of it for me to inherit when I turned eighteen. I would appreciate it later. Our little settlement was a blessing and the house was fuller like I wished.

On March 4, 1981, I turned six years old and had a lot of catching up to do. I was glad to be up and running and playing with my sisters and brothers. Hide and go seek was on. Victor was four years old and our baby sister, Lisa, was turning two years old this month of March 31. We were jamming it up, running up and down the stairs to pop music.

One day, there was a small tornado and mom told us we had to go in the basement to find shelter. I hurried first and ran to the window to check it out and to my astonishment a huge ball of wind was approaching fast towards our townhouse, snatching up everything in its way, such as small trees, garbage cans, etc. I was shocked to see such a whirlwind which was very huge to me.

However, after we sheltered in the basement for a while, mom said that it looked like the tornado passed by our house. I was *relieved and felt very safe after looking out the window to see our old 24th St. Vliet Street looking nice.*

Father was gone all the time. He would be hanging out with his friend, Al, who lived down the street from his parents' house. Some occasions he would carry my brother and me with him.

I enjoyed it when he would let us play in a nearby park. My dad would play basketball; he was a very good player. While my father was running up the courts, Victor and I would be swinging the swings and swimming in the pool.

Chapter Three
Family Chaos

Our typical family life took a dark turn. Father began to come home agitated and argued excessively with mother. And he began to spank us over anything. On one occasion, he was yelling with my mom in the room and when I passed by, he was slapping her in the face, making her cry. I was devastated and ran in my room crying. I hated it when I saw him hit her for the first time.

The next day, I watched mother do laundry and I noticed the hurt in her eyes. I wanted to comfort her but I was too young. My support was nothing. She needed her sisters. However, I hugged her.

As the days went on, I noticed changes in our family atmosphere. My dad and momma began to argue more frequently. I reasoned upon myself that since the family was under pressure, I had to take responsibility as the oldest. I realized that my mother needed help and I was capable of helping with some of the family chores and my sisters' and brothers' wellbeing.

One day, I was sweeping the kitchen floor and before I looked up, a hard whip went to my butt. My father whipped me for no apparent reason. I was devastated and ran to my room, hollering, and crying. I was not used to his hardness. I felt like he didn't like me. I used the word like, instead of love, because love was a more meaningful word and he did love me. He was just frustrated and for whatever reason, he took out everything on me.

Things didn't get any better. Our home became more and more hostile. My dad began to beat my mother more. Finding out my father's mother had passed away; he took out all his anger on his family. My dad's mother didn't really like my mother because of their marriage and he was her youngest and spoiled baby boy.

Victor and I shared in my mom's and dad's fights. He began to beat my mother and also whipped us. One day, my brother and I were walking up the stairs and my father came in through the door and just started whipping us for nothing. Next, he went upstairs to the bedroom and started hitting momma and I heard her yelling. I got scared and Victor and I were still crying from our own bruises.

Yet, I was the oldest with the most strength and courage. I ran to my parents' bedroom. To my surprise, I saw the unexpected; my father was slamming my mother against the wall. He was pulling her hair and she was screaming and yelling, "Stop, Victor!"

The next thing, he rammed her head into the concrete wall and what was left of the wall was a large hole. My father really did it this time. He cracked her ribs, and momma was screaming and crying for days and was without medical help. I was traumatized by her hurt and shame.

Mom was just standing by the kitchen table crying, and very hurt. I remember hearing the brokenness in her voice Because of the loneliness and despair she was in.

I hated myself, for being so young, I was very intuitive. I had great insight and judgment to be a seven year old young girl. Our home was too chaotic, that was my judgment as a young girl. Everyone in the house, except my father, was certified physically abused. The trauma of being abused affected my mom and we missed days at school. We would just stay at home.

My dad punished me more because of the decline of house duties that were assigned to mom. However, because of the abuse she went through, she had become heavy laden. So I alone was given the responsibility to complete the chores.

That's where my pain began and the severe interruption of my childhood took place. It hurt me deeply! For instance, he told me to clean the restroom and I did the best job I can do. However, he saw a few red ants and said to me you didn't clean the bathroom right, and he began whipping me with that large, brown leather belt. I hated it, that belt hurt! It became my worst nightmare for nearly seven years.

I wished my dad's mother had never died. He was too hateful toward us. Being the oldest, I had all the responsibility put on me. I had to clean the house; I had to watch all the kids. My sister, Lisa, had to trail me around whenever I went outside.

One very hot afternoon on a Saturday, Lisa fell down and scarred herself. My father physically abused me because of Lisa playing around too rough. I felt it was terribly wrong of him. It was cruel. I felt he hated me and wanted to be out of his marriage.

My mother changed her behavior. It could have been because of her physical abuse. Momma was not very social with us anymore and she was always in her room. When I did see her, she acted very strange.

Later that day, I had awakened from a nap and wandered into my mother's room. I saw Victor and Lisa sitting on mom's lap and I ran to get on her lap as well. To my surprise, she pushed me and told me I was too dark. I may have been young, but I was intelligent enough to know what that meant. I was lesser than all of them. I didn't deserve her love because of my color being darker.

My mom had a very fair complexion and my sister and brother were fair skinned with a honey complexion. I was an olive brown tan with medium hazel eyes. When I got older, I developed two other tones; my other tone was a powder fair complexion and a golden medium honey.

I considered it a blessing later to have inherited my mom's beauty. I thank the Lord for blessing me. Without him, I would have suffered tremendously with a negative self-image.

On the contrary, it hurt because my skin wasn't as fair as the present. However, I carried this trauma from my mom's sarcastic remark and behavior for many years. It hurt me deeply, and I just ran in my room crying my soul out.

Why do people show such cruelty to others because of their skin not being light enough? I guess it's one of the wiles of Satan. The devil just got angry because he is not light anymore. He was cast out of heaven and became the prince of darkness.

I believe he differentiated God's lightness being represented as good and better while darkness as evil and lesser. So it's a great coincidence that people differentiate color like Satan does the power of light and the power of darkness. Therefore, being darker you're less, and being lighter means that you're better.

Many people live with demons every day and are unaware of their demonic presence. This Satan theory is just my opinion.

My young life was saved. My aunt, Christine, came by and saved our lives from my father's madness and my mother's dissociation with life. Aunt Christine noticed that mom had a nervous breakdown and called the paramedics immediately.

We were all sheltered into foster homes through child-protective service. I stayed with two older people for about one day. Victor and Dwayne stayed with a foster family as well, because they were teamed together. Lisa was in a foster home on her own.

The next morning, social workers moved us with our family members. I was glad I was placed with my grandmother right away. My brother also stayed at my grandmother's house. Dwayne stayed with my Aunt Karen. Lisa stayed with my Aunt Christine. We were all safely housed and away from my green eyed dad.

During my foster home stay, I met two of my best cousins and great friends Tiffany and her younger sister, Claudia Haessly, whom are biracial. I love them sooooo much. I remember one of the best moments we had was when we were dressed alike with red shirts and leather black pants singing "Say, Say, Say" by my favorite artist, Michael Jackson.

The latest news on my mother's health, according to the talk around my family, was mom suffered a nervous breakdown. My mother acquired a very serious mental illness called Schizophrenia, which was a very critical condition for a beautiful twenty-five year old young lady. Apparently, she walked around with a broken rib, and pinched nerves.

It was 1982, and I was a seven year old, who had seen the gates of hell all within a year. After my father's mother had died, my dad became a monster to us all. He turned into Mr. Hyde and hated his family. We were his number one enemies. That's why we had the terrible accidents. However, I thank Jesus, that we were blessed to live somewhere peacefully, until my dad could find a better way to release his anger.

I felt guilty for not telling momma I was okay about our recent fuss when she refused to hug me because of my skin color, favoring my dad's. I had some hidden resentment from my hurt towards her. I wrote a letter to myself, telling mom that I forgave her and that I was sorry for her accident, and that I still loved her. I wish we would have stayed in Pontiac, Michigan, and mom never would have gotten hurt.

In the beginning of the year, momma had swept us off to stay with her grandmother. We hid there for a couple of months and attended Jehovah's Witness services on Sundays and also their assemblies. It was a warm visit and I loved the jelly sandwiches that my great-grandmother gave us.

Then one day, dad came with a friend and picked us up. Now here I am at grand mama's house and Momma is at the Milwaukee Mental Health Complex. I had to adjust too many different transitions and my life and this was one of them.

Grandma said that we will stay with family until my father completed all his anger management counseling sessions and a judge would release us back into his company.

Momma was hospitalized for about three to six months. I soon began having visits with her. Mrs. Janice Yancey (mom) looked very well. Her hair was combed in a style. Her clothing was very *conservative and mom's shoes matched her purse. I loved my mom I wished we were home again and all these terrible things never happened.*

The chaos of our family environment had been squashed. Exactly eighteen months later, we were back at home.

Six months later, momma was pregnant with her last child, a nine pound baby girl named Kimberly Lynette Yancey. Her birth took place at our new residence at 1338 N. 24th Street, on the west side of Milwaukee. Father had deleted the thought of physical violence from his mind.

A lot of things took place here. Me and my sister, Lisa, received perms for our hair. We attended many different places with mom, such as shopping and going to the zoo. Lisa and I shared pop music together and watched music videos on cable.

Our family ties were strengthened by love, communication, and quality time. I graduated from fifth grade. Our theme song for our graduation was "The Greatest Love of All." I was proud to have graduated.

Chapter Four
Discovering My Youth

I completed elementary to everyone's satisfaction. I entered junior high with a breeze. I was a young girl about to experience the sway and the source of the pre-adult years. I was very happy to begin class. Momma had to catch the bus with me to show me the route to school the first couple of days. I was a little timid entering class the first day.

The kids at Robert Fulton were welcoming, yet a few pranksters were there. I was one of the victims later to get mocked. I put my talented skills together and turned my mockery into a comedy show and I had everyone laughing at my jokes. I was glad they found me amusing rather than to rank on my three shirts I wore every three days.

I asked my neighborhood friends to loan me clothes so I could appear middle class with lots of stylish clothes. My friend, Deborah, had clothes she could not fit anymore. I was given about six outfits; some were from her older sister. I even visited grandma and she gave me some nice used clothes and bought me a couple of new outfits including shoes.

Father was very poor; he no longer worked but received low income assistance. He received SSI disability income for mom and my younger brother, Dwayne. Our income totaled $1,776.00 a month. Our duplex cost about two hundred dollars a month. My dad gave momma an allowance of $375.00 a month. He gave me twenty dollars a month for allowance and ten dollars to Victor and Lisa.

Dwayne was only four years old and Kim was one year old when I began the sixth grade.

I became popular in my sixth grade class and as I mentioned earlier, I became a great comedian. Everyone enjoyed me and started calling me by my last name, Yancey. I was glad of my new popularity. My low self-image of feeling inadequate slowly left. I had past image problems about myself. I felt my eyes were too little and my head too big.

My comedic skills brought me overnight popularity. I felt good about being Miss Yancey. However, it didn't affect my love for English. I was very intelligent in reading, writing, and spelling. I mastered spelling words and I received B's and A's on all my spelling tests. My dad was proud when he came for parent conference classes.

I made a big difference than my fifth grade experience. When my father would visit my fifth grade teacher, Mrs. Washington, her report on me was a minor report and dad was displeased with the below average grades and yet I did improve in her classes with a C+ average.

However, in sixth grade junior high, I improved with an overall B average. I loved school, yet I still felt timid when I walked through the hallways and passed by the seventh and eighth graders. I felt their advancement in age and experience as junior high school students a little bit intimidating by them.

One of our classmates was named Corinthia. I greatly admired that name and asked her where her mother got that name from and she said it was biblical. The name was from the book of Corinthians of the Holy Bible. I said that one day when I have kids; I would name my daughter Corinthia Marie Yancey.

The next school year I advanced and was a little more developed. My grandmother put a curl in my hair and it made me prettier. Momma had exposed me to skin care with Noxzema which gave me a new brighter skin tone. I had attained a golden yellow complexion. Mom also bought me some pale red lipstick. I managed to make it look nice on me by dapping a little on very gently.

However, the many afterschool visits to Aunt Michelle's house showed me the fashion life about the glitz and glamour of modeling, makeup and fancy clothes. Aunt Michelle taught me how to wear eyeliner. Michelle was a local model, her fiancée and kid's father was a painter and decorator. He took many fancy photos of Michelle and used some for advertisement. He was hired by many retail businesses to design their ads and Aunt Michelle appeared in many of the ads.

Her dream was to become an Ebony fashion model. Michelle loved classic movies and mimics Joan Crawford from make- up to mannerisms. I watched a lot of classic movies with her. I love Joan Crawford and Betty Davis. Michelle shared with me how she lost her dream in the seventies of appearing at Joan Crawford's former studio called, MGM.

Aunt Michelle was very beautiful; she had a high golden toffee complexion like me. She was about five-feet six inches tall like my mother. I inherited both of their heights.

I would spend days off from school at Michelle's house watching Sparkle. I favored Irene Cara. She caught my attention as a sweet innocent baby sister who modeled her older sister. I was smitten with the love relationship between her and Michael Thomas. They were very beautiful. I had hope of one day experiencing an undying love as theirs. I would always favor Irene Cara throughout the years.

I went to school one day, with my new look of Egyptian style eyeliner and the kids hovered over me. They praised me for how pretty I had become and for my fair complexion. They were used to the golden toffee brown complexion.

I received fame in my seventh grade year. I had a new best friend that I had acquired in math class who was very attractive and famous with the boys. . I also became popular with a lot of guys. Everyone was screaming our names. Every guy wanted to hold my hand.

I felt my new friend was beginning to be a little too fast for me, especially because of what I had been taught by mom's religion. I felt guilty wearing all the make-up and flirting with the guys. But, I soaked up all the attention they gave me.

After school when I would go to the grocery store with my neighbor, many guys flirted with me. I remember on one occasion, I was told that I looked better than Janet Jackson. Some of the flirtation I received was very negative; I attracted adult men that were from eighteen to about thirty years old.

One day after school, I was stalked by a man who appeared to be about thirty. He followed me from my home to my grandmother's home which was a distance of about fifteen blocks. He stalked me there and all the way back home and even waited until I came back outside. I had next gone to Sentry's Grocery Store which was about five blocks from our home of 24th St I was not sure why I saw this same man. I said it must be some type of mistake. I said when I left the grocery store if this same man was still following me I was going to ask him why was he following me? I had a mean-spirited side I inherited from Ella, my great-grandmother.

To my terror, this man was waiting outside the store as I left. I was terrified and began to run a little. As I got a block away from the store, I turned around very angry and asked him, "Why are you following me, you got a problem?" The man walked up fast towards me saying, "Yeah, I got a problem!" And he reached towards my neck and I screamed so loud that he took off running. I was hurt and traumatized by this.

My thirteen years of age was very challenging. My popularity became somewhat of a curse. My blessed beauty I had acquired had gotten me dangerous attention, the stalker, the older men making passes at me, and the jealous violent girls.

One day at school, they had to end classes early because of a tomboy girl that wanted to beat me up because I was pretty and chatting with young men in my science class. I became the victim of many fights.

Two neighborhood girls befriended me and one whipped my butt twice. The first time it was in front of my house. This girl was deranged and she had tried to beat me in the hallway entrance of my house but my neighborhood friend pushed her away from me and kicked her butt for me. However, this crazy girl returned and demanded to fight me by myself. So I went downstairs to fight her because she irritated me. I wasn't a good fighter. She swung at me continuously and I felt the blows of her hands. I tried to swing as fast *as I could at her but I was too weak. I felt a little sick. Her family broke it up; they were standing there watching the fight the whole complete time. I suppose my friend was scared to help this time. I had another fight with her while I was dating my first true love of junior high.*

On one occasion, I had almost got beaten by one of my neighbors that also attended school with me. This girl's name was Darkena. She was a healthy girl and had a secret grudge against my skin color. One day, I was coming out of Darnell's house. He was a platonic male friend. Darkena and about eight girls met me on the lawn. She had crutches in her hand and rushed towards me trying to hit me and fight me. I was smart and I ran very fast home. In fact, I out ran them all, made it to my house and rang that doorbell repeatedly. Within seconds, my dad opened the door and saved me.

I missed school a couple of days with my father's permission. I felt it was the solution until things died down. When I returned to school, Darkena had apologized. I was safe once again to walk the halls.

Furthermore, home life was okay. Mom and dad were happily married and I daydreamed over the idea of getting married one day as they are.

After dinner, I announced to them, "When I grow up I want to be a wife, mother and a model." My dad laughed at me and mom said you're still very young.

I met my first teenage love rather early. A sixteen year old guy named Christopher Hughes. A little bit older than I, he attended South Division High School and worked. He was very handsome. He was about five-feet tall with a nice muscular shape, a fair complexion, and very dark alluring eyes. I was very into him. I would watch him go pass our house on many occasions and I decided one day, I was going to catch his attention.

On a sunny day in the summer, as I talked with my friend, Deborah, I saw Christopher walking towards us and I decided to stand in his way with my hand on my hip and smile at him. He stopped and noticed me and we hit it off from there. We exchanged numbers and I talked to him by phone every day.

I would listen to a song called "I Need Love" and it reminded me of Christopher's charisma. With this guy, I learned the beginning of dating. He was respectful and took me out on several occasions to the theatre and restaurants. When he returned me home after one of our dates, he gave me a romantic kiss that made me fall in love, however, it was infatuation and I was too young for love.

I visited him at his home after school one evening and as I sat on his lap, he began to kiss me with passion. I felt special, like I never wanted to go home again. However, Christopher was moving a little too fast. He wanted to go all the way with me. I was still young and carried my parent's morals.

Christopher got upset and was slightly physical with me; I was hurt by his aggressiveness. Why had he become pushy and made me feel like my body was more important than me as a person? I left and said I would talk with him later.

After many telephone conversations with Christopher, I decided to see him again. We went to the show, then over to his aunt's house and there I let him take my virginity. I was in love with him and I trusted him with my mind and my body.

After the experience, I was relieved. I felt like a cool girl. Some of the girls at my school had passed the flower of their age and it was deemed cool and popular.

However, shortly after our breaking of the law of the land, we departed. I wrote him one farewell letter telling him I was too young and it was infatuation, and that school was more important to me. He had written me back and said he wasn't ready to get serious with me. And that one day we might meet again when we're more mature.

Summer love was over and school was back in session. I was an eighth grader and it was the last year of junior high. I felt free having no boyfriend and hanging with my junior high school friends again.

I spent my summer being a little selfish. I strayed away from some of the girls that I attended school with and usually talked with on the phone. During the summer, I was always writing letters to Chris and dreaming of him. I made everything up to my friends.

I was back to normal, I felt guilty betraying Jehovah God and his son Jesus. I asked mom how I could be forgiven and she said ask him in prayer and confess your sins. I did just that. I made a firm dedication to her to wait until I am married to have sex.

I met a lot of new people at school during this new term. I was embracing English class splendidly. Our learning topic was a dramatic literature script from "The Princess Bride". The script was very creative and mysterious. The teacher was very patient with me and let me read much of the literature. I became very fond of it and read it with great enthusiasm. There was also a film of medieval literature. I enjoyed the film very much. I was enchanted with it. I maintained a B average in English.

My science class boosted my self-esteem. I created a good hypothesis of a scientific matter; it included a detailed multi drawing of the hypothesis. I felt good and was on the right track. I felt young and wholesome again.

However, the curse was still on and I was still the devil's target. The curse was a generational one that Satan put on descendant after descendant. I was too young at that time to know the exact details of what all my family curses would be. The enemy, Satan, lays out cards for people's lives. What he laid out for me so far was oppression which now included teenage pregnancy, poverty, and physical abuse.

I met a young man named Obadiah at a friend's home. I had met him briefly the year before. He had made a pass at me then but I had refused because I felt I was too young and he was too old; being a junior in High School. However, now he was an eighteen year old who had completed high school at North Division.

I liked his appearance and his personality. He seemed intelligent. He was an average height and very attractive with unique Cherokee Indian features. It was love at first sight. He was a charming person and wooed me right off of my feet. He was very friendly and asked me a lot of questions. I was nervous in his presence and felt immature at some of his questions.

When we met; I gave him my address, and he gave me his. We talked on the phone sometime and I visited him almost every day.

Sometimes, Obadiah picked me up at home and we went to his home. I had many dates with him and they took place at his home. I was pressured daily by Obadiah for sex.

I had felt abuse from my last dating relationship. I heard all this talk at school and on television of guys using girls for sex. I was certainly a girl that hated to be used. But Obadiah made promises to never hurt me, saying that I could trust him, and that he would never use me. He stated he was in love with me. I felt right away he was my soul mate.

We were only dating about eight weeks and I was unsure about us. I wanted to end it but his charisma kept me into him. This man made me feel love and security. I felt safe when he held me; I felt I could tell him everything. I shared myself with him by giving him my body. I was shamed after I gave myself to him and took a four day absence.

Our next visit, he was happy to see me and felt loved for me. By the end of Christmas, I was confirmed as his main and only sweetheart and we were in love. His family respected me as his girl. I was proud to be his because I felt he had much popularity and respect.

We started having fights. Tom began to act possessive with me, and argue excessively over other guys I had only walked by throughout the day. He would ask me questions like, "When I am not with you, who have you been with?" He was very jealous and beat me up over his paranoid jealousy. One of his first abusive fits was in the kitchen of his parent's home.

One day there were a few friends sitting at table playing cards with him and I came down from his room to watch him play. He looked at me very mean, like what you are doing here. He got jealous of my presence around his friends. He took a piece of meat, smeared it on me and tried to get his dog to attack me. I was made to look very cheap by his cruel insecurities; he got jealous because I was very beautiful to him.

He also grabbed my arm roughly and squeezed it tight and I felt some excruciating pain. Next, he forced me into the basement and physically abused me more. I cried for days at this new strange behavior he had attained. I felt unloved and had acquired anxiety over our relationship. I wondered how we would make it in the future because of this big fight.

I had so many worries. I had noticed that my stomach was getting bigger, my period was late and I had pain in my back. To my surprise, on a visit to the doctor, I was told exactly why I had missed my period. The nurse said congratulations, "You're having a baby." I was shocked as I had forgotten that you could get pregnant from sex.

On the other hand, I was happy and couldn't wait to tell Tom the news. I wondered if he would do the right thing in marrying me! I went over to Tom's house immediately and showed him my pregnancy papers. I was shocked at his behavior; he told me he was happy for me. I did not like his answer. He could of have said something nicer and more detailed. I left crying my eyes out.

I had so much stress on my shoulders. I didn't know how I would break it to my parents, especially my father. I thought everything through and decided to tell him on his payday. I went to him my dad and showed him my pregnancy papers that I had received from Planned Parent. My dad just smiled and called mom saying, "What? Oh my goodness." I kissed dad for not whipping me.

I went to my room, laid on the bed staring at the wall, feeling hurt and betrayed by Tom.

I was ashamed to tell my grandmother. She had this good girl image of me. In-fact, my whole family did. I just didn't know how to break it.

I spent a week away from Tom and had no more overnights with him, or skipping school lying in bed with him watching television shows.

I stayed in the house and did not go anywhere. I made my dad happy by being home...He was putting an APB out on me when I missed dinner about three or four days consecutively.

I was adjusting to being out of Tom's presence. I was upset with him because he hurt me badly. He did not care, he just said that he was happy for me and left out the door. His lack of communication put a damper on my emotions and I suffered anxiety over him and being pregnant.

I talked to mom about my pregnancy and she went over doctor plans as far as which doctor would be nice. And Dr. Matson was my general practice doctor. Mom took me to my appointment and he gave me a routine checkup and then referred me to an OB/GYN specialist, a physician that specializes in the care of pregnant women.

Family ties were important to me, so I told my grandmother about my pregnancy and she responded in disbelief. She was very troubled and asked why I had gotten myself in this mess. I said it was an accident and was going to deal with it.

After my conversation with grandma, the news of my pregnancy spread all across the family. I had many visits from aunties and uncles. My aunt Christine insisted that I go for an abortion. I told her, "Definitely not, I love my soon to be child." I felt she was to be a special child and I was to name her Corinthia Yancey. I gave her my middle name Marie.

It was February 14, 1989, I went to visit Obadiah and I gave him a Valentine's card. He was happy to see me and he expressed it. He gave me a hug and a kiss. I told him how far along I was pregnant and that I planned to attend a school for pregnant women called Lady Pitts. I lay on his chest feeling loved and special. I asked him about getting married but he said he wasn't ready. He was too young and had a lot more to learn. I took the letdown okay. I wanted everything to be perfect and for him to compensate for my early pregnancy. I had a decent conservative image but getting pregnant early made me look bad. I looked like a hot tail bad girl to my extended family. It was sort of a shameful experience.

I had plans in the future of getting married at the age of 23 thru 27 after completing college. How and why did this happen to a beautiful young girl? I wanted Tom to make it right. Getting married and being responsible was the only solution to fix my life. Yet, I was too young to get married and the earliest I could wed with parent approval was 17 years old.

I was upset with Obadiah but most of all hurt. I accepted everything he had to offer and I didn't want him to leave me. I hated feeling rejected by him even though Obadiah told me he cared about me and the baby. As I started spending nights with him again, he became abusive. He would fight me over anything and anybody. His insecurity got out of hand again. The fights were painful. Some days, he would choke me and hit me with his fists in my head repeatedly. He would twist my arms and I hated that. It was scary and it felt like my arms was about to be torn from its proper place. Some days, I would run from him and he would catch me and finish beating me.

Over the next three to four months, this guy became my worst nightmare. We loved each other some days and then other days, I was severely physically abused by his jealousies. He put a gun to my head and said, "I'll kill you if you leave me."

If he wasn't around the house and I was talking to family and there were males around, he would hurt me for being around those men even if they were family.

One physical alteration we had, he started hitting me in his room and I ran from him. He caught up with me and threw me inside of a deep freezer and locked it on me. I was screaming my soul out for help. After fifteen minutes, he came in and got me out. The abuse seemed to get worse and worse. I was hit with ice shovels and left with purple bruises on my leg.

I was scared from this and I later developed Post Traumatic Stress Disorder, Clinical Depression, and General Anxiety. I cried for many nights, feeling I was going to lose my child from the abuse and stress Tom was putting me through. I suffered very badly, whereas I wanted to die. I felt so isolated when I returned home and declared it was over with Obadiah. It was May 1989 and I missed many days of school. I felt cheated getting pregnant by a psychotic loser.

At my parents' house everyone was doing okay. I disliked the environment and wanted to move in with my grandmother. Her home was more comfortable and richer. I did not want to raise my baby at my parent's home.

One day, I asked my father if I could sign Princess Kim up at a neighborhood school and he said, "Yes." I wanted to do this to gain experience as a mother. I went in, filled out an application, and they told me she had to get a routine checkup. So I took her to our family doctor and she got her shots.

I had one of my neighborhood friends press her hair. Her hair was very long and pretty; her hair was down her back. My little sister, Kim, had Asian eyes; she was a healthy, sweet girl. I took her to school and I picked her up. She attended a head start program for six weeks in the summer.

On the other hand, I needed money for my soon to be child. So, I took on a part time babysitting job that was sponsored by Milwaukee Public Schools. I received minimum wage pay. It was a summer only job and I was thankful to God for helping me obtain money with this job.

I had to work hard this summer. Being a pregnant woman was difficult for me. I had to attend summer school because I had missed too many days during the early part of my pregnancy. I completed summer school very promptly.

My environment changed because I and two other siblings had to relocate to grandmama's house. My dad started beating mom again and he got out of control with my brother, Victor. He was hitting Victor in the face and all over his body with an extension cord while he had stitches in his leg. I began to cry in sympathy for him and my dad turned around and whammed me in the head. I almost fainted.

I called the cops on him; they took me to get checked out at the hospital. I checked out all right. I was then taken to grandma's house. I didn't care for the painted living room that I had painted.

I was finished with my parent's home. Momma had brought my soon to be little girl a white flowered bassinet and it stayed with them as well because she did not want it to leave the house.

September came and I was enrolled in the ninth grade. I was glad to say I was in high school; it looked slightly better than being pregnant in junior high.

My due date was October 4, 1989. I had one month to go after starting school to have my baby. Grandma had bought me many maternity clothes and cradles for the baby. I was ready to bring a blessed, beautiful child into the world. It was okay to bring her into this world; I didn't need to have anyone's permission. I said if the Lord would forgive me for my sins and bless her as his then through the Lord, I could be a spiritual virgin again, and I was.

Furthermore, on a Tuesday morning at school, I began to have crucial pains in my lower back and I said I must be in labor. I went to see the school nurse and she said she doubted it was real labor; most people don't have their baby's on their due date. I told her I must be in labor, so she told to breathe slowly. She checked my heart and my baby's, and told me that I could complete school. However, by midday I was still having pains and they got worse. I could hardly bear it. As soon as I got home to grandmama's house, I called the paramedics because the pain was hurting me so badly.

The hospital rejected me and said it was false labor because I had to be dilated a certain amount centimeters to get admitted. So my aunt, Karen, came and got me and took me back home.

Around evening, all the kids were gathered in grandmama's room watching Annie. The pains were getting more crucial. Aunt Karen came in the room, took one look at me and knew that I was in labor. She said, "Come on, I'm taking you to the hospital."

When I arrived at the hospital, I was immediately checked. They did an ultrasound and said I had not dilated enough to be admitted into the hospital. But my Aunt Karen insisted that I be admitted. I was shocked that I was not considered to be in labor. They sent me home again and Aunt Karen gave me some orange juice. I vomited all in her car. I was very appreciative of her kindness and patience.

It was a difficult situation. I had to endure a lot of pain. I began moaning and about an hour later, she took me back to Mount Sinai Hospital emergency room. They completed another ultrasound. I was filled with a lot of water so they couldn't even tell what sex I was having. However, I was dilated enough to be admitted. It was Oct 3, 1989 and around 11:30 pm, I was safely admitted in the hospital. I thanked the Lord for his mercy and kindness. I was in labor for about twelve and a half hours and it was hectic for me. I had my labor pains in my back instead of my lower abdomen.

My Aunt Karen had put in sessions of applying a hot rag over my back to soothe the pain. I was sighing inside, "When will it be over?" My daughter, Princess Corinthia, arrived at 12:00 pm, the day of Oct 4, 1989. I was blessed, delighted, and humbled to bring a healthy seven pound ten ounce baby girl into the world.

Everyone came to see my baby girl. All my aunts were there, my grandmamma, and cousin Wimpy. My Aunt Christine bought me a couple of nice gifts for the newborn baby. I was very thankful of her support as well; she had also given me a nice baby shower when I was in the early part of my pregnancy.

The physician whom delivered my child was very prejudice of me. He had a problem of me being under age and pregnant at fourteen years old. He took a very long time to begin my delivery; I laid there in pain and agony. However, it was time to deliver my pride and joy, I pushed Corinthia out with a breeze and my worries were all over. The doctor made a sarcastic remark, "Don't get pregnant again at fourteen." I say it was prejudice and insensitive.

The next nice moment was to see my baby girl. As the nurse handed me my daughter, I embraced her with love and warmth. This was a moment I will never forget, my special friend, and meaning that gave me an appreciation of the value of life.

I left the hospital and went to my cozy large bedroom of my grandmama's single family home on the north side of Milwaukee. My room was carefully prepared for the baby. I had my room thoroughly cleaned, carpeted, painted, child proofed, and new blinds. It was equipped with a nice cradle, swing set, highchair, stuffed animals, new blankets, and everything you can name.

I was certainly prepared to be a mother. Yet, I was a bit nervous. I had much experience with help raising my younger sisters and brothers. Even though I was young, I believed I could be as good of a parent as a twenty four year old.

The first week was all about nurturing and also a little stressful. She was spoiled right away, some nights she wouldn't stop crying unless I picked her up and patted her on the back and walked around the room.

I guess staying up many nights became a burden on my body and I developed some back pain and a fever. I had a setback and had to go to the emergency room. The doctors wanted to perform a pelvic examination while I had stitches and I told him it was too painful for me. I went home and healed my own setback using home remedies of chicken noodle soup, and Seven Up soda. This method helped the fever and the nausea and I also took Excedrin for the pain.

I was out of school for six weeks. I enrolled my daughter in a private home daycare. My main priority was to lose weight since I bloomed to 168 pounds at the end of my pregnancy. After the baby was born, I lost a lot of water but still weighed 151 pounds. My permanent weight I desired was to be 125 pounds, standing at 5'5 feet tall. I returned to Lady Pitts to complete ninth grade year.

The next three years, I lived with my grandmamma and my daughter. I adjusted to motherhood very well. I was looking into the future for Corinthian and me. My plans were to get my child's father back in our lives, achieve higher in my studies, and transfer to a regular high school for my tenth grade year.

I visited my child's father about eight months after she was born. I waited this long because I was broken hearted at the fact he left me for another woman who was now pregnant and because of the physical violence. He was happy to see his oldest baby girl. However, he was still with the other baby momma. So my plans of marriage were off.

However, I felt I could still try to win him over; I just had to wait a little while. I planned to get my own apartment by the time I was sixteen so maybe he would see that I was not just a little child, but yet a mature young woman who can handle a child and a home.

After I talked with grandmamma about Tom, I decided it was over for good. I would raise my child on my own. So the next five years were giving Princess Corinthia the best years of life.

I promised to give her all the love, all the attention, and all the hugs that I never received of from my parents. By the time my daughter was one year old, I had lost all my weight. I wore a size seven in pants and had a size 24 waist. I had restored my youthful shape and my radiant glow.

It was 1993 and I had turned eighteen years of age. I was planning my twelfth grade graduation with my grandmamma. I decided to go with a white limousine to usher me to the ceremony and then ride around three hours with a high school colleague who also graduated with me.

My Aunt Karen bought me a nice black lace dress with the back cut like a heart. I picked out a black and silver rhinestone necklace with matching earrings and ankle bracelet. I also picked three inch velvet pumps with diamonds cut around the edges and a small velvet purse. I had planned to wear my hair in a corn roll, with Shirley Temple curls all around in a mushroom bang style.

The day of my graduation everything went as planned. I walked across the stage happy; however, I felt a little cheated. I was missing one math test to receive my high school diploma. I was very upset by this careless loss. However, my guidance counselor told me I can still walk across the stage and graduate with my class. He stated I would just have to take the math test in the summer and receive my diploma thereafter. Besides, he said the students don't actually receive their diplomas during the graduation, but afterwards, by mail. I was ashamed of being short of the math class; however the bright side was I was graduating with my class, Amen.

My daughter, Corinthia, attended the ceremony and also rode with me in the limo for about one hour. My grandmother was there and my aunt, Karen, with her camcorder. My child care provider attended as well.

The post-graduation was simple and nice. My friend and I hit the restaurant drive through and ordered up some food. The limo experience was fun. This concludes my youthful days of learning, developing, making mistakes, and being submissive to elders.

Chapter Five
Isolation Days

The transition of being a young adult was rewarding but yet gloomy for me. I moved into my own two room efficiency apartment located on Milwaukee's downtown side. I obtained credit of six hundred dollars from a furniture store. With it, I purchased a two piece velvet navy sectional with large floral pillows, a black liquor five-piece dinette set, and three floor z shaped lamps, two were black and one was white. The white one I put in our bedroom. A floor size stereo system was put in the living room. I had a nice size picture window. I also purchased a twin brass headboard from a thrift store and a new twin size bed for Corinthia.

My grandmother brought me a white microwave for my graduation. A male friend, who was a nice confidant that I met some two years ago in high school, also brought me a nice housewarming gift. To my surprise, he gave me two rings, one was a friendship ring and they both were diamond 14 kt gold. I loved them it cheered me up.

A social worker where I attended living skills classes gave me a nice house warming basket filled with all sorts of things, and I really adored the glass vision pot set.

I was happy to have my own apartment and have no one bossing me around. I was free to make all the decisions about the house. I could cook whatever I wanted. I could clean whatever I wanted. And have whoever I wanted over. I could now further discover myself. Being an adult, seemed a little frightening for me. Even though I was truly delighted and thank God that I have made it this far, for my daughter and myself.

My first couple weeks were setting up the home, getting phone service and cable television. I loved watching movies of all sorts. My favorite movies were classics, such as "Splendor in the Grass," "Rebel without A Cause," and the "The Ten Commandments". I also loved watching "Mahogany" and "Lady Sing the Blues". They were very inspirational films that taught me about unconditional love and challenges that people go through. I believed some of my characters reflect the most creative inspiration of films.

I still had this yearning to be an actress, however, my first agenda was taking care of the home and raising kids. As the weeks went on, I started thinking about my failure of not passing the math class.

I felt deeply hurt and I started eating more and more. I also thought about how my child's father looked at me the last time I saw him. It was a disgusting look. I know it must be because of my looks declining and I gained twenty pounds. I was one hundred forty-five pounds and wearing size 10 pants instead of a size 7 that he had once treasured.

I developed a negative self-image about myself during this adjustment period of self-independence. I was very depressed because of the beauty image everyone had held of me and seemingly overnight it all had faded away.

I pondered over the failure of my math class and had anxiety about retaking the test. I was very confused about some of the algebra problems. I studied some of the problems and called my cousin, Tamika, over to help me.

By the end of June, conformingly three weeks now in my apartment and departed from high school, I began to sleep more and feel this sadness. I woke up and looked in the mirror and I did not like who I was. I did not look like the same person; the Dorothy Dandridge from Carmen Jones. The beautiful lady of class and delicateness described my beauty.

I put on eyeliner at the age of thirteen for the first time and from then on until graduation. Now I looked somewhat old and a little bit heavy. I was going down and a part of me really did not care. I started to dislike myself and I harbored feelings of inadequacy because of the intensive worrying and the feelings of hopelessness, consummates depression, and anxiety disorders.

My social life was abnormal. A month had passed and nothing had changed the way I felt about myself. I was isolated and stayed in the house crying a lot. I did not talk on the phone with my usual group of people.

It was the month of July and the family was planning a Fourth of July barbecue at my adopted Aunt Karen's house on 36th Keefe. I went out and bought Corinthia and myself a matching two piece short set and sandals. And we took the 35th Street bus all the way there.

My brother, Victor, had just got released from a long three year sentence for attempted arm robbery at a juvenile detention in Wales, Wisconsin. I had visited with him with my father and mother.

I remember going to trial with him and trying to advocate having him released when I was only sixteen years of age. I was a very brave, outspoken person. I felt I had the guts and intelligence as a college age woman. Victor appeared so vulnerable at the hearing and he cried most of the time at the sentencing. I went home in great despair. I could not handle his trying trial.

I felt like our family was just born to be full of troubles. I hated all of our bad luck. However, on the family visit I had with him, he seemed to be doing fine. He could have developed some nerve problems. However, Dad tried to make him happy the best way he could, with his hilarious jokes.

Furthermore, I was so glad to see Victor there and driving. I gave him my new address, and told him to pick Corinthia and me up sometimes. He had been one of Corinthia's favorites during my three to four year stay at grandmas.

My sister, Lisa, gave Corinthia a nickname, Rinnie, and my brother, Dwayne, nicknamed her Ren. They both started calling her those nick names a couple of years ago. I noticed Lisa & Rinnie playing very beautifully. The barbecue was videotaped, and lots of pictures were taken. It was sort of a huge gathering. Corinthia played around with the kids while I gossiped with mom, Lisa, and Victor.

I sort of forgot all my worries and enjoyed the moment. I wondered how I was going to get home, I guess I would ask my brother, Victor, to drop me off.

It was Thursday morning. I looked at my calendar to see what was planned for the next several days. As I figured, I was due to take my math test on the school board on Saturday. So I took out my notes and studied. I was a little pessimistic about it. I seemed rugged and anxious.

I believe myself image played a larger part when trying to achieve my accomplishments. I wanted to desperately change my appearance. I felt myself worth was determined by how beautiful I was. If I didn't look like much then I was nothing. Some days, I was so upset about how I looked that I did not want to go outside. I weighed in at 160 pounds. One of my high school colleagues mocked on my sudden weight gain. I was saddened that my appearance wasn't in no more.

I was disappointed at my weight gain. I knew I had been eating more because of my anxiety and excessive feelings of hopelessness. It came Saturday morning and time to take my math test. I was feeling too bad about how my body feels. I did not want to be seen by people on the bus. It was hard for me to function. I did not really want to miss out on this moment of having the second chance to obtain my high school diploma.

I called around to see if I could get a ride and a babysitter. No one was there to help me out. I took the lowliest way out and stayed in bed. I just took it all in and put the hurt behind me. I said to myself, there are other days; after all I was still young.

One day to my surprise, I got a visit from Victor; he came in the house dancing and acting silly. I was happy to have company. It cheered me up. I turned on some pop music, and Rinnie and I danced with him. We kept the dance going on.

I decided to turn on the TV and watch a movie called the "Inkwell". Corinthia loved this movie about a young fellow on the weird side who had some interpersonal problems. He was sort of a young mischief. However, it was a nice Black American family movie. Victor's visit was almost over. He said he was looking for a job to rehabilitate himself. Meanwhile, I continued looking at this film with my little girl.

My days were uncertain and my daughter's life was confirmed. I don't know where I am going but I do know Corinthia's life is destined.

A sudden tragedy happened in the family. My mom's dad passed away. He had a heart attack in his sleep and was found dead lying with his bible in his hand. I was not really close to him. However, he was my granddad. The plans for the funeral were for the entire family to drive by car in families of four or five. I teamed up with my adopted mom and my sister, Lisa, and my daughter, Rinnie.

I was still suffering from low self-esteem and depression. However, I managed to function at a level to speak to others. We were all off to Pontiac, Michigan; the drive was about eight hours.

When we all arrived, it was late, around eleven pm. Momma and Rinnie and I stayed at my great uncle's house. He had a nice cozy single family home in the suburbs.

It was a sad time for everyone. My adopted granddad was a well-known person and very well liked. I just socialized with a few distant family members and cleaved to momma.

The funeral was arranged by my distant relatives. After the funeral my transport party all headed back to Wisconsin. I was exhausted and feeling very bad about granddad's loss of life. I wished he would've had the chance to unite back with my grandmother. I know he probably was lonely living in a single apartment at the age of fifty-four.

Back in Wisconsin, I was somewhat thrilled to be back at home. I took a five day extensive rest because of my lower back pain and nerves.

I hated the apartment because it was too country for me. I pondered over whether to move or not. I became frightened by my neighbors. There were too many weird people hanging around downstairs, when I went in and out.

One day, my brother came over. I went down to let him in and an old man without any clothes on was trying to grab me and mumbling something I could not understand. I was angry and wanted to tell him off. My brother told him off for me and said, "You are disrespecting my sister and don't come in her face again."

Another day, an older man knocked on my door asking could he chat with me. He said he noticed me through the window of my apartment watching TV alone and figured I wanted some company. I told him, I remember you asking me questions a month ago. The answer is still, "I do not want to talk with you," and he left my door.

This man was ridiculous. On another day, I had my sister, Lisa over with me. We were all watching Malcolm X and the same weirdo was hollering across the way, waving at me through my open picture window. Everyone started screaming. I told them to calm down. That man came knocking on my door for the second time. I had it; I told him I was calling the cops if he comes over here again.

I started crying because I was too young for all this stress. I was only eighteen years old. I don't want to look like an old maid by the time I turn twenty five years old.

The next day, I went to put in a two week notice to get out of there. It was adequate time to find a more stable home. I called my Aunt Karen and asked her if she could rent a trailer and move me in a couple of weeks with some of the boy's help. She said she could do it; I just have to pay for some gas.

It was towards the end of summer and it was the day of moving. I had lots of help including my brother, Victor. My sister, Lisa's trailer was a large one but the move took two round trips.

My new location was a shabby area; I could not afford a nicer place. However, it wasn't like those thirty three complex apartments. It was a two family duplex on the corner of 46th and Lloyd not far from the suburbs called Wauwatosa.

This duplex was laid out much better. I had one large living room and a medium size dining room, a nice size bedroom, and a cozy kitchen. I decked it out with my furniture collection.

After I got settled in. I looked through my phone book and thought I would call one of my old friends. I called my sister's over. We grew up from 24th Street and we were delighted to talk to each other. To my surprise, she lived about three blocks from me. I invited her over and told her to bring a couple of male friends so we could play some cards and drink wine coolers. She was all for it. I made *the date for the weekend. I called my brother, Victor, and left a message for him to come by.*

A couple of mornings, my brother came by and even one of the days with his younger play brother, Mark. Mark was a young Jewish, Christian. He was a handsome, humble guy. His brother, Luke, was born on the wild side. Luke was sort of like my brother, Victor. They created spiritual mayhem everywhere they went.

They were the ones I believe responsible for breaking history. They helped spiritual blessing's take complete itself. The two tried to say it was Luke. However, I did not believe them. Luke was sensitive about the accusations.

Here it was Friday and my social day begins. I had the house all clean. I had some music going. I had my little sister, Kim, over to keep Corinthia in the room. I loved my daughter and didn't want her to ever feel out of place.

All of the guests showed up. I had on some casual clothing. I looked averagely attractive. I was still 160 pounds. The guys were nice and somewhat social. The one I talked to was very quiet. He really wasn't my type. However, I managed to make the evening. Lisa was very friendly. We all played spades. I enjoyed all the card games. My brother, Victor, came and spiked the party up. I had to stop Victor from harassing Lisa. He started using I don't care. I got sick and I ended the party.

Victor was the last one to leave. He started arguing with me asking why I got in his business all the time because I was not his mother. I told him to leave my house. The next thing I know, he punched me in my face, and I ran to the stove and threw my nice vision glass on the floor.

When he left, I started to cry I was so sick of people hurting me and putting their hands on me. I was back in depression again. The hopelessness was gone for a second. Now, I'm back in the darkness. I made a self-loathing vow to have no communication to anyone by phone or in person. No one could skip school over here. I told my sister, Lisa, to tell everyone I was serious there was to be no more skipping school.

However, I had my daughter enrolled in the same daycare since she was born. I said its fall so Corinthia and I are going to lie around, watch movies, and eat our junk food. We watched cartoons together. I made peanut butter cookies for us both. I had missed Corinthia throughout the day and was happy when she came home. I would give her a big kiss.

One day, I was feeling very lonely and I picked up a small hand Bible I had on the dresser. I read Psalms 91 and it was very comforting. I wondered how to get close to God. I thought of the presence I used to feel when I was younger.

I am broke! I need more money. I was receiving child support money of $478.00 and my rent was 285.00. I paid $25.00 towards security deposit every month. I had to pay phone bill and cable bill. I spent my last on food and household supplies.

I decided to go to the area library before my baby got home. I wanted to look up acting and childcare books.

I had got a call from a guidance counselor who advised me to take the math class and also an Infant and Toddler course at Milwaukee Area Technical College. He stated I could receive a certificate for this course.

However, back to going to the library. As I was crossing the street, a twenty dollar bill hit my face. I was glad. I said, "Thank God. I needed some change." I went into the library and looked up my information. They had some nice books. I checked out acting books that dealt with the method of acting. Some child care books on learning how children develop emotionally.

When I got home, I called Arlene Wilson Talent Agency. I asked her could I come in for an audition. I had a desire to be an actress. I was not happy with my weight; however, I said I will go as I am.

The day of the appointment went well; I gave her a photo of me. It was a nice photo. I was holding a red flower and it looked very dramatic.

The talent agent, Carol, gave me good reviews. She said I was a natural actress and she was signing me on as a newcomer on a temporary basis. She told me to send her about twenty-five black in white photos. Carol also told me to take some classes for acting. However, she decided to give me one of her very experienced actresses to give me private acting lessons and voice lessons.

When I got home, I was screaming for joy. I can't believe how fast I got accepted into a Sag Union Agency. I read from the acting books, how it was important and also the first step towards a career in acting.

I had a second unexpected financial blessing. I had gone to the grocery store and as I crossed the street, I noticed a twenty dollar bill again. It was the Lord blessing me in a peculiar way. He was providing my needs. I was a single mother and raising my kid alone. But yet, I wasn't alone. His shadow was all over me. (Amen).

We were all a little click (sibling's & daughter) that hung around each other at family gatherings. I had a depression problem and this really set me back. I moved out of my house and back to grandma's. I was terrified to live over there. I hated criminals. I said the next place I will move into will be suburbs.

I don't care how long it takes to find it. Going through grief, it really hurts. To cheer myself up, I went shopping. I bought Corinthia a beautiful, large doll house. I was back in my old room again. My sister, Lisa, was still living there.

1994 was approaching and I needed a new outlook. I got a call from a subsidized suburban apartment complex in Glendale, Wisconsin. I had to walk a few blocks from the city bus. I went and viewed the apartment. It was very beautiful and neat. I wanted to make this move quick and possible. I looked at a local newspaper and hired some movers for $50.00.

This suburban apartment would be my permanent home for the next eight years. It's a place where I discovered my young adult life. My grandmother told me in a joking way "to get out and take your sister, Lisa, with you. I am tired of you Yancey's." I was excited when I moved into this apartment. I purchased a sofa bed for Lisa. I also had to purchase living room carpet from Menards. I decorated the apartment with class. I had floor size mirrors attached to the walls of my living room and dining room. I bought large plants to put throughout the house. I received a school grant and added to my furniture list and clothing list as well.

I enrolled my daughter in a suburban school. I completed my MATC class. I also passed the math test and received my high school diploma. I was nineteen years old and life was looking up again. The Lord was truly blessing me.

I ran into a conservative friend that I used to chat with from my neighborhood home. She was working and living with her mother.

I was accepted in an associate degree program of Child Development. The following courses were college level. I enrolled in three courses at MATC. I took English Writing 192, Advanced Reading 100, and also Health and Nutrition 100.

I had an audition with Arlene Wilson for an industrial film. I went in and auditioned by videotape. I told Carol I was working on the black and white photos.

I was very busy and blessed in this new apartment. Corinthia's birthday was coming up and I planned to give her a party at Chuckie Cheese.

I purchased a journal and begin to take note of my life. I was very interested. I found the Lord very gentle and understanding of us as a people. I was drawn to him.

I obtained a Jewish program...an Inspirational film...I could say that I got saved; I was a new creature in Adonai Yeshua...(Christ; Jesus).

The film was very testimonial.

I have overcome my days of isolation.

Chapter Six
Being Born Again

It was 1995 and my second year living in Glendale. . Corinthia and I were adjusting well. My sister, Lisa, decided to move out of the apartment with her aunt- in- law, Gwen. However, she stayed in touch throughout the years.

Day by day, I got more interested in reading the book of John in the Holy Bible. I wanted to reinvent myself. The word was the answer to renewing your mind. The word gave me peace and hope. I read and read until I passed out one day. I realized how serious life was and that I could not beat my weakness that had been plaguing me on my own. I needed help and God was the only answer.

I had been in darkness all my life and I had been acquainted with abuse all my life. I said to myself, who can deliverer me from this mess. I started a detailed research into being born again.

I watched TBN about five times a day. They had so many different religious programs. I almost did not need to go to church. The church services that aired on TV were big name pastors like Pastor Marilyn Hickey, and Evangelist Joyce Meyers, Billy Graham, Evangelist, and many more.

I watched a Jewish program with many Rabbis' and I wanted to find the solution to getting closer to the Lord. I viewed many testimony services on this TBN channel. I cried daily to the Lord and asked him to save me and to fill me with his Holy Spirit.

I don't want to be in darkness. I don't want to walk around with a crutch. I want to be set free. I came from a family with some bondage and some curses. They were in bondage to sickness and diseases, physical violence, poverty, and mental illness. I felt hopeless about my unsuccessfulness in life.

It seemed like when I prayed all the devils in hell came to attack me. I knew if I could feel his presence then I was truly having faith enough to receive his Holy Spirit. I wanted the fullness of his spirit. I had great awareness that his Holy Spirit was the only entity that would bring a massive change to my person.

I had a struggle with myself and no one knew about it. I was in isolation a lot because of my weight gain and raising a child alone. I had a negative self-loathing view about myself because of the physical abuse that plagued me and the rejection I felt from it.

I had several relationships and they had not ended the way mother's was. She got married and I did not. However, all my relationships ended in rejection. Yet, I was still very young. I had to just pace myself.

The end of 1996 was approaching. I had not accomplished much and I needed a change. The year of 1997, I planned to give myself to the Lord. I yearned to be free from depression; it was robbing me of my life.

I believe it was some dark curse on me with men. However, to make life a little more interesting, I would eat and watch love films. I was the natural escapist. I ended up having an eating disorder. If anything didn't go right; for instance a job loss, argument with family, or anything that causes great distress, I would be comforted by food.

Each time I prayed, I felt nothing. I was trying to get closer to God to feel his presence.

My Jewish friend told me according to the Bible, I was saved. I wanted more. I met several young, Christian women that had organized a Bible group. All of them were chosen; and they were educated enough to know about being born again. They told me to study John Chap. 3.

According to John Chapter 3:3, a man named Nicodemus came to Jesus by night and said to him, "Rabbi, we know that you are a teacher come from God; for no one can do these signs that you do unless one is born again, he cannot see the kingdom of God." (John 3:3 KJV) Verse 4: Nicodemus said to him, "How can a man be born when he is old? Can he enter a second time into his mother's womb and be born? (John 3:4 KJV) Verse 5: Jesus answered, "Most assuredly, I say to you, unless one is born of water and the spirit, he cannot enter the kingdom of God. Verse 6: "That which is born of the flesh is flesh, and that which is born of the spirit is spirit. (John 3:8 KJV) Verse 8: "The wind blows where it wishes, and you hear the sound of it, but cannot tell where it comes from and where it goes. So is everyone who is born of the spirit." (John 3:8 KJV) Verse 16: "For God so loved the world that he gave his only begotten son, that whoever believes in him should not perish but have everlasting life." (John 3:16 KJV)

I meditated on all these scriptures every night. To sum up the subject of being born again. For one to gain access to the Kingdom

Of God, one must be baptized by his water and they must also receive his Holy Spirit, Amen. (3:5 KJV)

The natural man is corrupt in nature, he was born in sin and his desire was towards sin. Therefore, we must appreciate the gift of being born again. It's deliverance of the soul, bringing it into the eternalness of the holies of holies. Furthermore, the natural man must become a spiritual man in order to understand the things of God. That which is spiritual is spiritual, and that which is carnal is carnal.

I was excited to turn 21 years old in 1996. I had a small gathering with my sister, Lisa, and my cousin, Tamika. I made some hors d'oeuvres. I entertained them with one of my Christian films by a Jewish church. We had a nice time.

One day, my Jewish friend also invited me to a restaurant called Manning's. I stopped in there with them. It was a very small crowd. I saw this guy staring at me and I smiled at him. He walked up towards me and said, "Hi, what's your name." I told him I was a Christian and just here at the request of my family. That there are certain things I just don't do. He said, "Happy Birthday!" He asked me what church I went to. I told him Christian Faith. His name was Richard and he told me he attends church sometimes. Even though he's not a regular, he enjoys it when he goes.

I told him I just got born again. I invited him to church. He was delighted at my offer. He made me blush. I told him it was nice meeting him. He grabbed my arm and asked me for my number and if he could take me out for dinner.

I said, "Certainly, I have no problem with it." The party at Manning's was great. I went home feeling important because I had family come over and show me a good time. I had a guy make me feel attractive.

I picked up Corinthia from my dad's house. I stopped and bought some laundry detergent and Corinthia some of her favorite gummy bears. When we got home, I prepared for the next day. Corinthia was in grade K5 and I had to get her clothes and mine out for the next day. Being a single mother has its ups and downs.

After I completed the household chores and put my baby to sleep, I laid in the bed thinking about my life. I started to yearn for God. I got on my knees and started praying for the fullness of his spirit and to speak in the gift of tongues. I wanted to make sure I was born again. I prayed to the Lord to bless me with a male friend.

However, he gave me a scripture to seek the kingdom of God first and everything will be added. As I prayed, I started feeling a strong mental block again so I started praying more earnestly.

Friday morning, I woke up and I felt terrible and did not want to go anywhere. I said if anybody calls, I am not answering the phone. I was thinking about how the devil tries to oppress women.

I hated the devil; he made me weak at times especially when I wanted to achieve things. I slacked at a lot of things. In the last two years, I couldn't hold a job settling for very low income. I tried several jobs and they just did not work for me. I remember, I got hired at Glenview Nursing Home. I lasted only five days and when I was pressured by women to gossip, I walked out.

Later in the afternoon, I received a call from Richard. He sounded delightful. He asked me what I was doing later. I told him nothing. He asked could he come over and study the Bible with me. I was all for it. I told him, I was being very devoted to God. He said he's not trying to take my God away. I told him how I was seriously in love with Jesus.

When Richard arrived, he gave me some flowers and a hug. I said to myself he is so sweet. I wonder will this lead into marriage. I looked at his beautiful, starry hazel eyes. He came in and I told him to sit down. I offered him some tea. I asked him what study in the Bible he would like to get into. Richard said he would like to read the book of Galatians.

I couldn't believe I met a guy that has a church background and actually showed up on time for the date. Before we began reading the Bible, Richard asked me all sorts of questions about myself. I answered every question. I liked this guy's personality. I told him we could take turns leading each verse. I was glad Richard did not say anything about my body. I wore a size 14 dress and a size 18 pants. I had gained a little more weight instead of losing. In two years, I lost only five pounds.

However, he commented on how beautiful my face was. He loved my smile and my hazel eyes. Richard stood about 6'0" feet tall. He had a muscular build and a low haircut. His clothing was casual. I asked Richard when he could come by again. He said whenever you want me to.

Six months have passed, and I'm in love with a Christian guy that treasures me. I can't believe we made it this far. Our relationship was strictly platonic. I thanked God for this friend He made feel like a person.

However, I was waiting on him to pop the question and I hinted at marriage. He said, "It's good you mention it. Give me your hand." I gave it to him. He got down on his knees and put a small blue marquise sapphire with two diamonds on my finger. He asked me if I would be his wife. I said, "Yes." I was screaming and crying at the same time.

I hurried and called grandmamma and I told her my long awaited dream came true. I am about to get married. She said, 'What? To your Christian friend? Grandma said, "What you mean you have been waiting all your life. You're only twenty-one years old. I told her that I had wanted to get married from the age of seventeen. Ms. Simmons congratulated me. I was glad to receive her blessings.

The next person I called to share the news with was my momma and my dad. I called my dad, Gae. Momma said he was around the house somewhere. I told momma about my marriage plans. My mom was happy for me and I told her to tell dad.

He was grumbling something in the background. I heard him saying, "Ah no she didn't." He got on the phone and said, "Wait a minute. Who are you marrying, not that tall guy you brought over here before?"

I said, "Yeah dad, and I am happy."

He chuckled and said, "That's nice." I was glad to have my parent's blessings.

I went through my address book calling everyone and then I said to myself, I am being too boisterous. I told my daughter about our marriage news and that she would have a new father.

It was Monday afternoon and I decided to call my agent, Carol, at Arlene Wilson and to ask if she had any leads. She said business was running a little slow as usual. She told me to give her a call in a couple of weeks. I took two sets of black and white pictures, for a total of twenty-five, and mailed them to her overnight express.

I got a call from Richard today, it was Wednesday. He sounded strange and said, "Mrs. Yancey, can I spend the next three days overnight with you."

I paused for a second and thought it over and said, "Why not? We're getting married." I love this guy, he lights up my life. I was so lonely before him and had many failed relationships. I started thinking when I will have this wedding. However, Richard was coming over and I hurried to make sure the house was well cleaned.

We spent three nights in bliss, but I hated he made me commit fornication. I told him God was strict, that we have to honor his word, even if we plan in the future to obey his law by getting married. We must stick to it no matter what the cost is. I told him that I felt very guilty of committing this sin.

One time was enough and he has to be patient if he loves me. He agreed with me and said he will not stay over pass nine o' clock pm. I loved Richard and there's nothing I would not do for him; however, I loved Jesus more than anything.

We spent the holidays visiting family and lying watching classic movies. We also had the bliss of candlelight dinners and listening to moonlight piano music.

By December, I had a bad fall out with Richard about my body. He told me he wanted me to lose weight by the time we got married. I told him that's rude. After all this time, my weight started to be an issue with him. I said, "How much you want me to lose?"

He said, "About fifty pounds."

I started crying because he was being insensitive and selfish. I just said, "Okay, I will work on it."

One day Richard was over, helping me reorganize the house. He asked me to sit down, he wanted to discuss something and I sat down. He asked me how much weight I had lost so far.

I said, "Nothing."

He said, "I wanted you to lose at least five pounds by now."

"I said, "Are you all right? You don't sound very Christian; it has only been one week and a half."

He looked at me very angry and slapped me hard in my face. I pushed him and then he started grabbing my arms tightly, and kicking me on my legs; saying, "I can't stand you! I hate you." He was crying and dragged me around the house to the bedroom. I was yelling and screaming for Corinthia to dial 911. I kept telling him to leave me alone and get out.

He said he made a mistake, in asking to marry me. I felt like I was wounded in my heart at the echo of those words. I was lost and screaming get out of my house. He had no right to play games with my mind. I said, "Why did you lie to me?" as I was crying my eyes out. "What is this? You beat me over my weight."

He started yelling, "I don't like for a woman to cheat me and tell me she will do whatever I told her and then not do it." The next thing he started forcing sex on me. I felt like I was a piece of meat and he was a very sick man.

I thought I knew him and he loved me. He betrayed me; I hated myself for allowing him in my life. I wish I would have left him at that Manning's restaurant. After the fight and rape, he said he's sorry, kisses me on the cheek and left. I lay in the bed wanting to die. I was ashamed of my mistake. I hated my body; I started crying and thought about killing myself with a bottle of pills.

I was hysterical. I did not know what to do with myself. The pain was so deep; I could not comb my hair, take a bath, take my daughter to school or even walk.

I call my sister, Lisa, and told her what happened and that he tore my soul out. I started crying, "I can't live anymore." My whole being felt like it disappeared. I felt distant from God. I was ashamed to talk to him and yet selfish. I felt it was sort of his fault, because he could have prevented this. I said on the other hand, the Lord was probably showing his father's side and looking over me. The Lord just interfered to make a lesson out of my male relationships, once again.

God always breaks things up. Why did he let him hurt me? I am grown. I can learn on my own. I know God is my father but sometimes he is too overprotective. I felt God spoiled me too much sometimes and then he whips me too much. I have had many chastisements of the Lord. However, it's okay to receive them and it's an act of his deep concern for those he loves.

"I never want to see this man again," I said to myself. Two months passed and I got what I wanted. I never saw him again. He was an evil man.

I lay in bed very depressed and despaired. I turned on TBN and I heard a pastor preaching a message about a man lying in the pool of Bethesda for thirty eight years and an angel would come in trouble the water and Jesus comes up to the man and said, "Will thou be made whole?" (John 5:1-7 KJV) The pastor went on to say, this man always had excuses for thirty-eight years and the man responded to the Lord, "That whenever he tried to get into the pool, someone would beat him and step in first." The Lord said, "Rise, take up thy bed, and walk." (John 5:8 KJV)

This poor man had made excuses for thirty eight years. I can say as for me, I have made plans to do things and have not completed them. I said I would stay away from people that abused me and yet I find myself back in their hands. How long shall I suffer? Those words stayed in my mind. I have been broken down spiritually and lost my self-esteem. I was not going to think about my situation. I was just going to get up and walk in faith.

I was standing up, picking up my bed, and walking. I didn't care how hard it was. I didn't care how long I had been in despair. I was not going to think on those things that upset me. I was going to stand up. Out of all this pain and shame, I was going to have faith that I can be healed in Jesus name, Amen.

I decided I was going to have to fast for about three days. And ask the Lord to fill me with his Holy Spirit and with tongues. I had fasted with only water for about three days. I said I was going to do something out of the ordinary, and this was it, fasting. I prayed earnestly with my whole heart, mind, and spirit. I cried out to the Lord. I said, "Your word is your word, and you do not lie. You are a God of truth, and a God that hears the cry of your people. How long shall I bear this burden of bondage? How long shall I live in complete darkness? I want to be made whole again. I want the pain to leave my memory. I want to be filled with your holy spirit. You said if I ask, you will hear me. If I knock you will open the doors. If I seek, I shall find. Lord, hear me, and fill me with your cloven tongues. I want you in my life more Jesus. I don't know what to do with myself. I can't bear it alone; I got to have your love, and your kindness."

I suddenly felt the Lord's presence over me. This was a sign that he heard me. I made a proclamation to continue in righteousness and witness to my family and neighbors always.

About two weeks passed and I was baptized at Oak Creek Assembly of God, Apostolic Church, in March of 1997. I turned twenty-two years old.

It was about 9:30 am and I thought about why it was taking so long to receive the gift of tongues. I asked Jesus, (Yeshua), why he has not answered me. I have done everything, what else was it that I shall do.

I turned on the radio, listened to some worship music and I began to say, "Thank you, Jesus, Halleluiah!" I repeated this prayer of showing gratitude and showed my love for Jesus. I began to meditate on the Lord as the divine, omniscient God, and repeated, "Halleluiah", over and over. Next, the beautiful Holy Spirit just came to me like a baby being born and like cloven tongues of fire. It welled out in a beautiful heavenly tongue. I could say I was truly a part of God's kingdom now. I was very blessed to be a born again Jewish, Christian. I had the gift of eternal life. I was covered in his blood, (Yeshua).

I began a journey into the deepness of the Lord's character. I changed churches and started going to a Jewish Synagogue. The head Rabbi was a prophet and so was his wife. I believed going to a smaller, spiritual, Jewish church would help me grow in the spirit better. This Jewish prophet prophesied to me that I was called into a fourfold ministry. He said your family rejected you, but you are the Apple of God's Eye. He said, "Many bruised you, but the Lord said, 'I found you'."

This confirmed why I kept receiving the Deuteronomy scriptures of God's Covenant with Moses. The main point I received from this scripture was that I am a prophet. The Lord revealed to me the covenant that I am to receive these blessings if I would keep the commandments of the Lord thy God. You will be blessed in the city and blessed in the field. (Chap. 13 verse 4). Ye shall walk after the Lord thy God, and fear him, and keep his commandments, and obey his voice, and ye shall serve him and cleave unto him. (Deuteronomy 12:28) Observe and hear all these words which I command thee, that it may go well with thee, and with thy children after thee forever, when thou doest that which is good and right in the sight of the Lord thy God.

I developed a closer relationship with Jesus. I discovered my gifts; I had the anointment to preach the Gospel. The Lord gave me the scripture according to Jeremiah Chapter 1 verse 4 KJV... *before I formed thee in the belly, I sanctified thee, and ordained thee a prophet unto the nations.*

I could say, having Jesus, I saw generational curses being broken. "The Devil is a Liar!" I have completed many things and experienced many blessings. Here are some of the accomplishments I have achieved. I organized a Bible study group with some family members and also chaperoned them to church and back. I was more giving and I showed more love. I began completing a business plan for a child care agency. I attended a business seminar and then I hired a professional business writer to complete my business plan. This was how the Lord blessed me out of bondage. I was blessed with more knowledge and wisdom. I lost about fifty pounds. I felt good about my self-image.

I completed about a semester of upper college courses. The English 201 (Public Speaking Course) was a favorite of mine. I had so many successes after being transformed. I also attended some theatre courses in Chicago, Illinois. I had plans to one day start a theatre and my ministry.

I was blessed to be healthier in my body and soul. I had been saved for about three years. I was turning twenty-five years of age in March. I evaluated my life and said I had a lot to thank the Lord about. I had my shares of up's and down's throughout the years, but I made it.

One painful experience I had to go through was losing memories that slightly tarnished me. However, the Lord helped me. I could say being born again was a blessing and a peace to my daughter and me.

Chapter Seven
Driven in the wilderness

(GOD'S Silence)

I had achieved my goal of receiving Early Child Care 1 and 2 certificates. I began work as a head child care teacher at the YWCA. I received a nice amount of pay. I was delighted to work for this company. My daughter would attend work with me some days, when school was not in session. I enjoyed Corinthia and my teamwork with the students. I had a small group of students, ranging from the age of two and three.

I continued my studies in college. Time used to be an issue with me. Now, it was meaningless to me. I take each day as it comes, thanking the Lord.

The year 2000 was approaching. I was turning twenty-five years of age. I was restored by God and born again at twenty-two. Nearly three years had passed and I needed to find ways to become known as a woman with a high calling in the five-fold ministry. I had not progressed the way I should have. I had much knowledge and insight. I should have had members and an active Bible study going on. I felt guilty and I believed I was a little selfish. I should have prevailed like Jeremiah with a new bold message. However, I developed a struggle with myself that I could not get over. I was afraid to speak in front of a group of people.

I kept getting this guilty feeling that I was not performing all that he felt I was capable of doing. I made excuses. One time, I was asked by a pastor of my current church to give intercessory prayer. But, I declined because I had a shyness problem.

The pastor also had me teach a child Bible study class and also do the prayer over the offering. They were moving me pretty nicely. It was a blessing for me to have those opportunities. I realized when I prayed over the offering that I still had some negative portrait of myself. I would get very nervous when I was in front of a group of people.

I loved the pastors there and they really believed in me. I was treated like a leader, like I was already walking in the office as a prophet, and a pastor. I had the call but I was not there yet. I could say I was the least of all seeds, waiting to grow up among herbs. I was told by one of my colleague pastors that I was just a little evangelist. I had enough anointing to spread the gospel.

There were so many predictions going on in the year of 2000. I heard a prediction from the pastor of an assembly church that the millennium was coming. Another prediction I heard was the rapture was coming. I was waiting eagerly for the year of 2000 to approach. I didn't believe it was the year for Christ's return. I had not seen evidence of the major earthquakes, the black sun, moon becoming blood, and every island moved out of its place.

Saturday was here already and I took note of a religious play, titled The Lake of Fire, at the Capitol Christian Center on the North side of Milwaukee. This theatrical play was about the torments of eternal hell of those not set free from sin.

I called my mom's house and asked if my younger sister and brother could attend the play with me. Mom said, "Yes, she didn't mind and my father was gone over to his family's house for the day."

I headed over to momma's house in my 1998, white four door Pontiac 1000 car. I picked up the kids and we went to see this nice play. The scenery of the play was very professional and dramatic. There were a lot of people there, more than I expected.

After the play, they offered all to come on stage in accepting the gift of eternal life. Kim and Dwayne went up there to get saved. I loved it the way they were thrilled about something about the Lord.

Christmas was one week away and I had the apartment all decked out with Christmas lights, pictures, holiday teddy bears, and a huge white tree with gold and red decorations. I went to Sears Department store and took Christmas pictures with Corinthia.

I had planned a nice meal for my parents and siblings on Christmas Day. I bought presents for all of them. I also scheduled a prison visit to my brother, Victor, who was serving an eight year prison term since 1994.

I received an unexpected visitor from one of my junior high school friends. I asked this person how he got my address. He said he got it from a friend. I told him I was strictly with the Lord. He said he only wanted to see how I was doing. I told him any business with me, will only be pertaining to the Lord. I advised him to attend church services with me.

This guy was very persistent in my friendship. I asked him to call me some other day. I said to myself, "I have no time for people from my past which is not saved."

I called around looking for a small business loan to start my own daycare services. I wanted to be my own boss. I liked to determine my own hours and set my own pay. I looked in to many different avenues. I dropped off my business plan with the Women Business Initiative.

I followed up after their review day, and to my hurt I needed a more detailed projection. The women said everything was well explainable for a new child care business. I took that information as a positive further future prospective; my business plan was pretty well completed. I needed to revise my financial plan for the next three years. I was a little bit spoiled and sometimes really bad on rejection.

New Year's Eve was here and my daughter and I spent it nowhere else but the house of the Lord. I planned this year to move independently in the Lord. I promised the Lord no more backsliding and going into darkness. The Lord revealed to me many prophetic messages; Ezekiel 24 (The boiling pot), Jeremiah 1 (The Ordination of A prophet), and 1, 2 Kings (The Miracles of Elijah).

The last three years, I had been saved and filled with the Holy Ghost, with cloven tongues of fire. As a destined prophet, the Lord had revealed to me some of my prophecies for a latter appointed day.

I gathered from this revelation that I was to walk in the way of the prophets of the Old Testament and my prophecy would be like Ezekiel's instruction of "The Boiling Pot" preaching a message of separation of the good and the evil, then telling the evil that they're scum (filthiness) has filled the air and then taking it to Jeremiah's message: giving the people the message of doom and destruction. The Lord revealed to me, I would have a double anointment. I would perform miracles as Elijah having many signs and wonders.

Jeremiah's commission was one of my masterpieces and how I was to be molded as a young prophet. I was very young, at the age of twenty-two, when I received my high-call.

Presently at the age of 25, I received a major revelation, similar to Jeremiah's commission of the evil that has taken place in this world; an evil that has rooted itself through some organization. However, I have no more relevancy of the nature of its order. The Lord said be not afraid of their faces and go tell the people who I am. That it is time to restore the covenant and reveal the hidden sins in your life.

I was terrified to perform this order because I did not have much experience and I felt I was too young. I got the Jeremiah scripture again and what my Holy Spirit revealed to me was, liken unto him, the prophet. Jeremiah said, "I cannot speak, I am a child." The Lord said to him, "Say not I am a child, for thou shall go where ever I shall send thee; and whatever I should command thee thou should speak."

I had a sad prophetic dream about my only daughter. The dream had revealed her being oppressed by the devil and taken out of my home. I got her back home in the dream and she was very different. I woke up troubled from this dream and wanted to know another's opinion on it. I spoke with some prophets, and their predictions were way off. This was the first of six troubled prophetic dreams of my daughter. I also had a dream of my daughter and I being severely oppressed by a huge territory demon, and we were both delivered. I liken these dreams to the prophet Ezekiel (24). As he gave his message, he experienced sorrow in the family, as a sign.

I believed my tragic dreams of my only child suffering and oppressed was a sign of the future of my symbolization as a mourning prophet in darkness.

One day, I was lying around while Corinthia was at school. The darkness returned that I had got delivered from. I became deeply saddened and anxious of my responsibility as a destined prophet. I started escaping to food again. I thought about fleeing to Hollywood and becoming an aspiring actress but I put on weight again. I said if I become an actress, I can use the pay to develop my ministry.

As the days increased, my inadequacy became more and more troublesome. I developed some interpersonal problems. I was terrified to perform in front of people. I had no confidence to begin work as a prophet. However, I felt guilty, that I was just being selfish. It was really no excuse I could have tried a little harder. I just lashed out on myself and started having pity parties that I am no good.

My increase in weight had me down in the house again. I indulged in classic movies like "Gone with the Wind". I became fixated on this movie and dying for the love of a man. I became deeply saddened that I was young, and never able to find a suitable man to marry and to be a father to my child.

I declined in praying and church due to my Clinical Depression, and Anxiety Disorder. I got so depressed, that I stopped doing my hair and cleaning the house. I lay in bed for days, crying uncontrollable.

I decided to call Roger Memorial, a private facility, to see if I could stay there for a couple of days. However, I decided I did not want to leave my daughter with no one. I even became paranoid that I was going to die at twenty five years old.

On the contrary, I called a physician to find service, and I got an appointment with a Psychiatrist. I went in and saw him. As I spoke to him; he wanted details of my childhood to the present. I began telling him about my physical abuse by my dad and my child's father. As I explained incidents of my father's terrible abuse, I started feeling hurt all over again as if it was happening presently.

After I gave him all of the details, the doctor sadly said I had Post Traumatic Stress Disorder, due to when I explained the hitting accident; I flinched as if it was going on right at this moment. I was feeling the trauma associated with the abuse all over again. However, the doctor didn't prescribe any medication but encouraged me to attend church. He said a lot of people find healing through religious care. I agreed.

I started praying again asking the Lord to come into my heart, and save me, again. I was ashamed to have departed from the faith, after I had tasted his goodness. I imputed Psalm 35 and my morning regimen as encouragement and word of protection.

I continued in some acting classes to soothe my wild free spirited side; a side I really should not have. I believed in the creative power as a positive growth to one's spirit. However, growing in the word of God was the first growth of maturing my spirit (Amen). I enrolled at *the Acts Studio and the Center Theatre. They had method acting classes. I would have to drive there twice a week, an hour away.*

This was the selfish mind, I developed that led me to looking for higher pay, and working around the wrong people. I was childish; I didn't always seek the Lord in everything. I didn't feel it was wrong to take a few acting classes. I also started looking for work to make more money. I was thinking of relocating to New York to find a long-term career as an actress and use some of the money for my ministry and childcare. I decided to look for higher paying jobs that would afford me a private nanny and a nice residential suite. New York was a very expensive place to live.

I was looking into investing five years in film and theatre. I attended acting classes with my daughter. One of my classes was a commercial class. My daughter gave a great impression on video tape. She was a natural. She looked very well like a kid doing a commercial for McDonalds.

I auditioned at several theatres in Wisconsin. I completed a church play with a long-term colleague of Arlene Wilson Talent. I was a handmaiden name Darah. The play was titled "Go In Tell" and it ran twice at Community Baptist Church. The play also aired at the women's prison, in Tahcheetah, Wisconsin.

I purchased salvation flyers for witnessing I kept feeling I was not pleasing God completely. I went out to the malls with my daughter. We both put salvation flyers on every car in the parking lot. However, I felt that was not enough to please God. I did not know where to begin. I prayed to him and I asked him for direction.

I attended Christian Faith Fellowship Church again. It was March, and the Pastor was giving a 30 day fast with water, juice, vegetables and white meat. It was a nice healthy fast. I attended service about two to three times a week. Part of the vast requirements was coming to church about three to seven times a week.

I prayed in tongues more earnestly asking the Lord to cast down every imagination that was not of him. I was praying in faith to have depression cast out of my life. It was a hard struggle to overcome this weakness of clinical depression and trauma associated with abusive relationships.

I ran into some family problems. It was my younger sister, Kim. She was fourteen years old living and still with my parents. Kim had begun to hang out with the wrong crowd. Her female companions were living it up on the streets of North Avenue in Chicago, soliciting their bodies. To my surprise, Kim was involved in this illegal activity. I had to drive to Chicago, Illinois on one occasion to pick her up from the county jail. Kim was a little embarrassed and silent about the whole ordeal.

I offered her solace in support by offering my home to her so she could rehabilitate herself. Kim was a little agitated and selfish about herself. She did not live with me long. I let her stay as long as she wanted. I told her about Christ and some of my shortcomings. I soon let her go her own way; I had my own life and my little girl to take care of. I took her back home and gave her a Bible, and some clothing. I said, "Kim I don't ever want to see you on those streets again, there are other ways that you can make money." I told her about the value of life. God made every creature perfect in his eyes.

However, I had my own to look after. I can't save a person that doesn't want to be saved. I prayed for her to one day find Jesus Christ and have an abundant life through him.

One day while I was spring cleaning the house and rearranging some books, I began having some heavy breathing and it got worse and worse. I drove myself to the hospital and I was put on an EKG machine and the nurse said I had abnormal findings. One of my vessels to the heart was not getting oxygen. They said I was too young to have an abnormal EKG. They admitted me for a night and put a huge IV needle through my hand. I started thinking of God and my life. The devil had me scared thinking I was going to die. He whispered in my ear and said "I am going to kill you. I know who you are."

The night shift nurse came to me about the Lord and said I was going through a trial and she handed me a book by TD Jakes, titled "Why Because Your Anointed". This book gave me inspiration and it helped me understand the trials you experience when you're anointed.

When I got discharged from the hospital, I picked up Corinthia from Grandmama's house. I went on bed rest for about one week.

I soon called my temporary employment agency for work. They had a position paying nine dollars per hour as a clothing inspector at a light industrial company for Harley Davis. I worked there about three to six weeks.

I had a hard problem trying to build up my blood. I went to the doctor and I was still anemic. However, I passed the health requirement for life insurance. I completed a fast for thirty days with nothing but 100% vitamin juices.

One day, I received a call from my grandmother telling me her boyfriend Frank's employer was hiring. She said they were paying twelve dollars per hour.

The company was not far from my residence. I went in and filled out an application. Several weeks later, I was called back in for an interview. They told me they would follow up and I would be called in to complete a second interview with the Human Resource Manager.

This company was the beginning of my sorrows. What I did not know was that I was walking into a job with a deadly secret. I had not enough spiritual light on me and I did not pray enough or even wait for an answer if this job was his will. I was young and unlearning in the word of God. I was still a babe in the word at twenty-five years old. I had not drunk the fullness of strong meat yet. My childishness caused me much grief in the latter end. Forsaking to putt God first in all you do has its consequences.

The horrors that were to take place was inhumane to my family. The prophecies that I dreamed about in the past were about to be revealed.

I was hired as the only woman of American Indian descent to be employed as an environmental cleaner. They had an African American male named Ted. We were the only minorities out of six Caucasian workers. I worked the first shift with four men and one female. Ted worked the third shift. At the beginning of the job, it was painful. The duties were too heavy for me such as cleaning large *dining rooms and cleaning about thirty bathrooms in the industrial area. I had to pick up large dumpsters by myself and toss them over. I had to clean office areas as well.*

I walked in this company as a twenty five year old single mother with one child; next I walked out as a twenty six year old victim. I was harassed right from the beginning of the job. I should have finished the job right away; however, I wanted to earn enough money to possibly relocate in the future. I felt something dangerous with this company, I was moving towards a dead end situation if I worked this job any further.

The Lord warned me in a dream one day that there was a man, an adulterer, and he was trying to make me a jezebel prostitute. It was Satan's deceptive device to attack God and turn his prophet into a liar. This man was evil incarnated. He was like the biblical end time Antichrist's twin brother. He was another man of sin that I had to be careful of. This man of sin started the increase spread of Satanism. He partnered with the devil, to help him gain control of the world. My grandmother believed he was the devil. The Lord said further in the dream that after this temptation of the man of sin, the end was near. Meaning this will be one of my last major temptations by Satan followed by the rapture of the church.

The secrecy was that there was witchcraft in the world. A cult that worships themselves and Satan...Information about this cult can be found on the internet.

Meanwhile, I filled charges with the EEOC and sought a restraining order. Yet, I was prejudicially denied.

As I fled the state, I became a target of the FBI due to the crime of bank robbery that my younger brother, Dwayne, had committed. He was only eighteen years old. I received a phone call from a federal agent to come into their office in discussing my brother's case.

The federal Bureau of Investigation tapped all of our family phones. They heard one of my ex-relative's "adopted" male cousin's phone conversations of attending a gun show. They detained him off of his conversation.

My brother, Victor, was severely beaten and framed while serving a previous case. The findings were Fed related. Several professional colleagues intervened and had the case dismissed.

My high call in the church and being a Native Hebrew woman made me a target of the FBI. The Federal Bureau of Investigation had members in The Church Of Satan, Los Angeles.

My family and I were being religiously persecuted by these two cults. The F.B.I. members that kept tabs on the Yancey's and my formally changed name Yocheved's.

They believed in the importance of Satan's dominance in the world. They believed his power was the source of all life. They entreated their devil worshipping as a religion. Therefore, following the beast doctrine of seeking to steal, kill, and destroy Christians.

The Federal Bureau of Investigation had denied our civil rights. They had slaughtered me as a prophet and a Native Hebrew young mother; claiming it's their job to destroy the works of the church as being obedient to Satan, as Christians are obedient to God. This *delusion of an unseen evil spirit that was really only in the Christian doctrine had manifested itself as a false religion worshipping the beast and religiously persecuting the saints.*

This rapid increase of Satanism was of the utmost concern. It needed to be exposed. It's a silence that has been remaining in the dark for years due to the strictness of the Constitutional laws. The FBI was afraid to bring it out to the light because there were still a few good people out there still. They still wanted to keep a conservative order.

Because this Satanic Cult was very traditional in its practice it believed in human sacrifice to gain power from the devil. This newly satanic doctrine that they hold was a counterfeit of the biblical Antichrist that was to appear some twenty something years later. They had secretly set up the system to follow the future order of the one rule, race, and religion, government that supposedly takes place years from now, when the man of sin is revealed (The Man of Sin) who is the Antichrist, who poses himself as Jesus Christ.

However, he was the beast according to 2 Thessalonians 2:1-4. He will oppose and will exalt himself over everything that is called God or is worshipped, so that he sets himself up in God's temple, proclaiming himself to be God.

However, we are governed by a system that was to be protected by the law. However, this system was being ruled by people that worshipped Satan and discriminated against Christians (especially leaders in the church).

I had been retaliated. Furthermore, my daughter has been assumedly forced into a gay lifestyle when she was illegally placed in a foster home in May of 2002 with foster parents in L.A. and six months later with a family. I was illegally placed in a mental hospital for one day and found to have no psychiatric disorder. However, they kept my daughter in the foster home system for three long years before I got her back.

Presently and tragically, my 19 year old daughter was heartbroken and put through rigorous religious persecuting acts. I have filed a complaint with the Cherokee Nation, Native Today; I filled a class action suit and a police report in Milwaukee, Wisconsin. But still no one pitied me. I have been in the dark for too long. I am the prophet that mourned for years in the wilderness.

I am currently about to appear on TBN television in the USA and India. I will begin prophesying the Lord's will and campaigning to rescue my daughter from the occult.

There were more details of my life being envisioned by the Church of Satan and the federal Government. Right after my daughter's illegal placement and my unjustifiable act of detainment at 2:00 am in a hotel in Los Angeles in 2002, I fled to Canada. I sought relief as a refugee in Canada against the United States, for crimes of inhumanity and tortuous acts of religious persecution. I had a Refugee Immigration Hearing.

The first place I checked into being a single women's shelter for homeless in Toronto, Ontario. Next, I visited an immigration legal office and spoke with an attorney about my US civil rights violation in Wisconsin.

One day, I decided to catch the subway to the west side of Toronto. I saw a sign that said, "Black Tie Event hosted by Johnny

Cochran". The attorney famous for high profile cases in L.A. I said this event was perfect for my situation. I would attend in hopes that my womanizing racial case in the U.S.A. would be heard and action taken on it.

I planned to wear a two piece black suit to look professional and very serious for the black tie event.

The day of the event was here. I gathered my 1964 civil rights brief complaint. There were many sophisticated people there and some were stars. I entered the event with no problem. I sat in the front row close to hear the speaker's. I noticed my immigration lawyer attended the event. He waved at me. I waved back!

As seats were filling up, a very tall detective looking CIA sat next to me. I was a little intimidated by his presence; however, I maintained my seat.

Johnny Cochran began to speak about many of his legal cases. Many innocent victims are framed by the Federal Bureau of Investigation and were tried and suffered long penalties of imprisonment. Mr. Cochran spoke of two persons. The first person was Geronimo Pratt; he was accused of murdering a school teacher. Mr. Pratt served five years in prison.

Mr. Cochran said that when he first met him and heard his complaint about the F.B.I framing him, he said, "He's crazy." Many others thought he was crazy as well. However, Mr. Cochran investigated his case and found it very worthy. Mr. Cochran sued the federal government and the case was found truth worthy. Mr. Cochran received five-million dollars from the Federal Bureau of Investigation.

I said this could be it for me. I have occurred the same misrepresentation situation with my case. Many persons believed that I was crazy, but I was not!

The next civil rights victim was Hurricane Johnson from the biography movie "Hurricane" starring Denzel Washington. I watched that movie many times and I love it! I was very encouraged by this film. The lecture event of the civil rights conference edified me. Mr. Cochran and Geronimo Pratt left the event immediately after closure.

After the conference, I approached Mr. Hurricane and his affiliates. I introduced myself as my native birth name Latosha Marie Yancey of Milwaukee, Wisconsin whom was also a victim of injustice of civil rights in the U.S.A. as a Native Cherokee. Mr. Hurricane was very courteous and straight forward. He listened to my brief complaint of my blue collar job and my racist harassment case that included multiple violations of the 1964 civil rights act. I was given a business card by Mr. Hurricane and told to fax my brief complaint to his office and they would review it.

I felt bolder and important after the black tie event. I added the title Political Activist to my professional self-descriptive resume. I decided to research issues of foreign nationals in Canada seeking asylum as a refugee. In the next week, I submitted more letters of civil rights violations pertaining to my family.

I had a refugee immigration hearing. The hearing was closed after one year due to reasons United States had enough resources to handle the problem.

I was homeless in Canada for about six months; from June 2002 until December 2002. My daughter was taken out of my care in May, 2002. I was on the streets in Canada with a deep wound in my spirit, and my heart. I can say I stayed homeless on the streets off and on for about three to five years through this wilderness phase.

I was vagabonding too many. I had a hard time with people on the streets. I developed diabetes, kidney diseases, and neuropathy, complications of diabetes (nerve damage). I have been sick with all these diseases for about five years.

When my daughter left my care, I strayed away from God. I became bitter at the circumstances. I was hurt real bad and broken. My home of eight years was lost. They evicted me while I was in L.A. seeking legal assistance in 2002.

I went to speak to a Los Angeles's district attorney about my harassment. I was seeking relief and to have jurisdiction transferred. The district attorney stated he would look into the case.

That following night, the police broke down my door and detained us. That was the last time my daughter had been in my care. It took me three years to get her back. I fought a long illegal child custody case with the state of California and the state of Wisconsin.

I asked my family to keep my apartment up and to keep my furniture. However, they lost the apartment while I was in the hospital and all my furniture was sold by the management of the company.

Eight years of furniture, photos, and memories were demolished. I felt lost and trapped in a system that did not care for the Hebrew,

Native race anymore. It seemed that overnight our race became the United States footstool.

The 50's and 60's minority racism seemed regenerated. Everywhere I went, I suffered racist cruelty. I suffered so much rejection that I was hurt very badly, and I could not function at times. Slight split minds caused errors of putting black Creole Indian over My Hebrew Multiracial Indian in some literature.

I had setbacks of depression, schizophrenia, PTSD. I was uncertain of my life and my daughter's. The question I asked myself was how long will we live. Will someone help us and will we make it out of this stalker's dangerous oppression. I know God will not allow the victim to be eaten up.

In my darkness, I had become a target of severe spiritual attacks by Satan and the victim of much witchcraft occult's and hexes.

I cried in the darkness because there were so many demons in my mind and around me. Some of them, they call "familiar's". Familiar's are unclean spirit's that a witch lead's. The familiar's follow the witch because they're her employee's.

I isolated myself in small hotels when it was convenient for me. Other days, I slept in isolated areas' all over the United States. For example a disastrous field, far out park and a neighborhood area against a large tree. Those isolated areas became my resting place when I was homeless for periods of two to three weeks due to poverty.

I yelled to people passing by to help me; I was in need. "Please help me; I am hurting." I put my hand out and asked many to have compassion on me.

Many evil spirits began to plague me from all the stress I was experiencing. My spiritual state became very dark. I developed into a state of legion - (person with many demons). The legion state was a severe bondage similar to the man of Bethesda by the pool whom laid in the same state for thirty eight years without yielding to the water's that were troubled by an angel for a bondage person's to be healed. During God's silence; the Lord spoke to me. The Lord asked me. "Do you want to be made whole?" The Lord said, "Do you want to go up to another level in my spiritual life?" I said, "Yes, Lord." And he said, "Rise up out of darkness!"

A Christian in a state of legion is too low spiritually. A legion state is a strong spiritual darkness hold where a Christian or any person is very low spiritually and far to semi far from God. These legion state persons are everywhere. They are people that are with severe illness such as Manic Depressive, Schizophrenia, PTSD and Multiple Personality Disorder with associations of demonic possession. These are very hurting persons. They have been living with this dark illness for a long time. God's light can heal you, you just have to go another level up.

I was forced to become a legion; an abused, isolated, rejected child. I developed a split mind. I had to die of the adult life I had become accustomed to. "Please, help me Jesus! Why doesn't my family love me, Lord? How could they let me hurt this long? Help my daughter, Corinthia, Lord Jesus." I sat for five-hours with my head bowed down and heard the mocking's of many witches. I was in pain.

I had throbbing, sharp pains in my head. I cried and cried and then I fell down to the ground. I heard a still small voice of a man crying, "Please, help me God."

I saw a vision of John the Baptist crying in the wilderness; the Holy Spirit empowered over me. I shared John's agony and pain and then I cried out to God, "Please help me out of the darkness." The voice of the Lord said to me, "I am come as a light to the world, and whoever believes in me shall not abide in darkness." (John 8:12) However, I held on in believing that God would make a difference, so I did not give up on him completely.

As the years increased and my daughter was gone out of my care, I began to lose faith more and more. I prayed to God, every day and the days just increased more and more. God was silenced during my exile; yet for a moment. He had made no major provisions in my life. I tried my own way of getting my daughter back and seeking justice. But no one had any pity on me. I attended church only about five times in five years. However, I prayed from time to time and started to keep the Lord's name.

After my exposure in Canada, I experienced rejection from my family more than ever. They stopped sending me the small allowance. I wandered around in bitterness. I did not understand why God had turned on me. How could my daughter have been taken from me and put into one of the worst foster homes in Compton, Los Angeles. My daughter was living with a lady and her fiancée whom was a false Christian. They abused her emotionally. I prayed for the safe return of my daughter. And began to ask God to forgive me for my disobedience since the year of 2000. I was selfish and not laboring steadfast of spreading a prophetic message of restoration for the lord and not giving more of myself to Jesus. My relationship with him was often corrupted by selfishness after two years of living right. By July of 2000, I made a mess of my daughter's life and my life. I should have been obedient.

I did know being born as a prophet was such a serious role. The Lord takes prophets and apostles very serious. I was called into the four-fold ministry. The Lord was not playing around with me. I hurt my family and caused this great evil to spread. I should have been giving the message of restoration and warning the wicked.

At twelve years of age, she left my care and at the age of fifteen, in 2005, she returned home, being accustomed to a lesbian lifestyle during her three year foster care captivity. I noticed a change in her; but she was still my sweet girl. I gave her all the love and all the affection. We had Bible study together. Corinthia would help me design Bible study for young women and childcare flyers for my Christian Young Women's Group for 18-34 year olds. We lived in a two bedroom apartment for about one year.

The year of 2005 everything was adjusting fine. I was glad to have my family back in place. Life had its up's and downs. We faced many challenges every day. I developed much character from my struggle. I acquired much strength to handle almost anything.

Furthermore, one day I discovered a secret that my daughter had kept from me. I found a group of notes that was written to my daughter by a female of her peers. It seemed of a lesbian relationship. The female was trying to pressure her into a serious commitment. I found another note my daughter had written replying that she wanted to have a normal life. That's she was not ready for that type of commitment. My daughter also stated she wanted to please her mom because her mom was a good Christian. However, I was glad to have her back home. I thank the lord for this blessed moment.

I told her that her lifestyle was important to me and I wanted her to be saved. However, I understand the human flesh and its desire. It craves to do anything against the will of God. I said to my daughter, I understand your hurt, loss, shame, and being a victim for three long years. I accept your lifestyle whatever you chose but I can't condone its right because of my loyalty to the Lord. On the other hand, I love you no matter what sexuality you choose.

One afternoon, I lay in my room all day while my daughter was at school. I reflected on my life. I decided to write a journal book about the hypocrisy of Christians. I titled a beginning manuscript "Are You Really a Christian?"

It was 2006, my daughter decided to run away and live with her girlfriend at sixteen years old. I was upset about this. She had only been back at home for almost a year, out of the three years we missed. Corinthia showed some strong dislike towards me. She blamed me for her abuse and severe suffering. It was my fault for working at a job like that.

I was upset by her leaving and her friend got the courts involved again. My sister, Kim, told me to let her go and live your own life. Kim lived downstairs from me.

I decided to move to New Jersey and seek assistance from a church and continue college. I called Corinthia's friend in notifying her to tell Corinthia that I was leaving town and if she wanted to go, to call my cell phone. Corinthia left a message saying, she's not.

I decided to let her go and move from Wisconsin. The Lord said to me by the end of the year it would become too dangerous for me. I struggled in New Jersey. However, I came across a nice opportunity to play an extra in an international film called "One-Nine" on a New York subway.

I was traumatized by the separation of my daughter. My daughter shared this as well. I talked to some pastors while in New Jersey; they insisted I return to my first love Jesus. And therefore I began preaching. I believed that if I would start to do these things, I would see the manifestation of his light. I would start to see changes in my life. I started to give God more praise; I worshipped longer and more earnestly.

I saw the heavenly of heavenly descend on me. God's light shined on me. I know I was doing the right thing when I felt the spirit of heaviness start to leave my presence. The Lord gave me an instruction to return to my first love and walk in obedience. He said if I start to make steps towards restoration, I would see all the dark areas leave and blessings restored. I said, "Yes, Lord; I will obey all your commands." (Amen)

By the end of 2008, my wilderness days were coming to an end. I had begun to preach, witness, and spread literature of salvation. I managed to stay enrolled in college for three years. I redeveloped my ministry website.

Every day, I spent long hours of prayer, worship, and reading the Bible. The Lord revealed more insight to me about my call, my life with my daughter and family.

I began to fast one to three days at a time. The Lord told me there would be some major changes to take place. I would start bigger projects in 2009. The Lord also revealed to me that my enemies would begin to perish. An angel of the Lord told me my main enemy would be rebuked from my life.

Being driven into the wilderness can be a most crucial moment for any Christian. I was purged and stripped of all myself. It was a painful experience to die to oneself. I lost all of who I was. The faded memories of my life began to wear out as I moved forward. It was the dying process of self. I spent many nights crying on somebody's hallway floor or on the floors of a hospital.

Some days I screamed madly while living on the streets with wolves. I also spent nights sitting at the bus stops; freezing and feeling the cold wind hit my face. I asked people passing by for money but they had no money.

I prayed to God asking him to save me from this night. I had to go through the night, but I thanked him that I made it. If it was not for him, I would have lost my mind or even my life.

Through faith, I conquered a super naturalness of his light and was healed of the legion state. No more pain. God healed me. I was sane again and was not bowed down in darkness anymore. God's silence was a test of faith for me. I was like Job; I kept the Lord Jesus' name. (Amen)

Chapter Eight
(The Apple of His EYE)
The Covenant Restored

After my struggle in the wilderness; I learned who the Lord thy God was. I was chastened for many years and suffered by his whip. I learned from the process of being stripped of everything. The period of being purged was a painful act of the Lord cutting all the rotten parts out of you and making you into his image, shaping you, molding your character.

Dying of oneself was a very sorrowful state of my person. I lost everything, my daughter, my apartment of eight years, my family, my friends, my health, and my finances. This loss of life was the cost of being the Lord's discipleship. I didn't really want to lose everything, but I was forced to lose my life in go through the wilderness phase. The word of God is "If you lose your life you shall gain it". I was obedient and gave up my life.

My testing and trials and the wilderness were a very painful experience. However through lost and rejection, I became obedient to the Lord's will. I was like Jonah in the belly of the whale. I had refused to act when he told me to spread his word.

Furthermore, while I was on the streets experiencing isolation of the wilderness phase I was in the midst of wolves. I began to cry out to the Lord for mercy and protection. Begging and urging the lost souls to repent of their sins.

To learn the ways of the Lord. He is not a God that is of a strange speech that you don't understand. However, he is a God of understanding that hears the cries of his people. It's not his will that any shall perish; it's not his will that we should be a heavy burden. However, it is his will that we should have life, and have it more abundantly. I bared my cross, and truly died to self. I came with nothing at the altar, and his temple.

I said, "Lord, I want to be in your favor again." And the Lord said to me, "Have faith and believe that even though you lost things that were precious to you, ye shall receive a lifetime of blessings." The Lord said, "Hearken when you hear my voice, and keep the commandments and ye shall receive the blessings of Abraham, Isaac, and Jacob. I promise you to give you a better latter end." The Lord said, "You strayed away from me as a wanton, greedy child to break my relationship off." Jesus said, "Return to your first love, and ye shall live." (Rev. 2:4)

I prayed to the Lord, more earnestly. I worshipped longer and I praised him more. I had been in a lot of pain and I know what it means to lose things. I appreciate the Lord's mercy and grace. Through the shame, I developed character.

God has kept his promise, he came to me with a mighty stretched out hand. He said, "You wandered too long, and you kept my name. Now I will spread my skirt upon you and show you the time of love. I will show you, I am the Lord thy God, who delivered you from your enemies."

Furthermore, my captivity was changed and the covenant restored. It is 2009, a New Year and I am looking at big things.

The Lord told me to walk out on faith and show me your works. He said look at big things this year. I started increasing my ministry by promoting it in a more open market. I redesigned my website and promoted prophecy's and sermons that I had completed on CD to finalize my struggle with myself and being rejected as a prophet. Becoming known as a prophet became my number one priority. A prophet has a high responsibility in the church. The Lord revealed to me that I will be one of his Watchmen in this last hour decade. A watchman gives the people warnings from the Lord. They are a prophet and his spokesman. They speak the words of the Divine God. The Lord told me I would be a special prophet during the period of judgment; where death and Hades take the lives of a fourth of the people on earth. This is the Fourth Seal.

I will forewarn the unbelievers and attack the spirit of Antichrist with fire. The Lord also revealed to me, I would temporarily lose my only daughter in this decade. It would be a sign liken unto Ezekiel when he lost his wife as symbolization during the great woe of the people. Many of the people had lost their children.

I had suffered the consequences of forsaking the ways of the Lord and seeking my own selfish way. When the Lord gives you instruction to go forth and show yourself as a leader; you must act immediately. I should have been like Paul, bold giving the message of the Lord to the people.

The Lord gave me further revelation in 2008 that after her return in my life for good a prophecy of a prophet who temporarily lost everything, my daughter, sisters, and brothers. Satan had me targeted on his top list. I would be a symbol as a mourning prophet who temporarily lost her only child. A woman with no excuse, suffering and made very weak but was raised to power. I will disarm Satan's camp with a vengeance. He stole my life and my daughter's life, my sisters and brothers. I would be a prophet on fire bringing much deliverance and healing through the name of the Lord.

During both of these seals, I will also gather the church and prepare them for the rapture. The main eternal blessed part that belongs to Christ. I will prepare his bride.

However, Satan wanted to destroy me. He did not want this mysterious prophet to be known. But thanks to the Lord, I have shared it on the radio. I like to share with my readers my prophetic message that aired on the radio Gospel 1570 AM of Chicago, Illinois. It's a replay of some of this autobiography.

This message is a glimpse of my crusade conferences that will take place in Israel in May, 2009 this year. We are living in the last hour. The Lord has given me a prophetic message. He said you will be my watchmen. You will perform what I have sent you to speak. You will be my witness to the nations. "Thus saith the Lord God; whomever will hear the word of this prophet let him hear, and whomever forbear, let him forbear. For they are a rebellious house. Yet shall ye know that a prophet has been among you."

The message that I want to share with you today is the upmost importance. A message that can save lives right now. That will make major changes in the world. I was called into the five-fold ministry. I received this call at twenty-two years of age. A single mother working towards my college degree, I had a problem with myself. I wanted to do things my way. (Here's my testimony) I became disobedient after years in the Lord. I had a fairy tale problem with being an actress and sometimes glamourous. Since the age of thirteen, I wanted to be a portrait model. However, when I found God, I declared entertainment wasn't for me. I got rid of this glamour delusion, and got certified to become a child care teacher at Milwaukee Technical College.

I had struggled all my life. My struggle was very crippling. I was born into a family that had been in bondage too many curses. Bondage to mental health problems, blood disorders, drugs, physical abuse, sexual immorality, and poverty.

I went through a lot of abuse in my life that I carried pain with me everywhere I go. I came from a broken home; I saw my mother get severely abused by my father and have a nervous breakdown. I was the eldest child and my father would put a lot of responsibility on me. I had to clean the house at only seven years old and be responsible for my younger sisters and brother's welfare. My father would abuse me on anything. If my middle sister got hurt, my father would physically abuse me. If one of my siblings messed up the house, I would get the beating.

I was in several physically abusive relationships. At thirteen, a very early age, I got beaten really badly by a guy about five years older than I. I got pregnant by this guy. He left me scarred. I developed post-traumatic stress disorder. A serious chronic mental disease and also a lifelong struggle with a tormenting weakness called clinical depression (considered a chemical imbalance.) This weakness hindered me throughout life. It was a struggle with me to keep a balance life and keeping stable homes.

My depression became darker as I got older. After I completed high school. I fell into a deep depression where I hid in the house for *about eight months. I could not function! The spirit of heaviness was on me so deeply.*

I had problems trying to concentrate with learning, when I started my first year in college. I would start nice jobs, and then just walk out on them; because of the negative self-image I had and the loneliness that plagued me.

I was the escapist; I would escape every problem I would have, by quitting everything from people, to family members, and relationships. If someone said one mean word, I would hang them up. I would carry it for days. My weakness was so tormenting for me that it trapped me to stay in isolation and to repeat cycles that led me in bondage.

I was never able to complete things. I never thought I could make it to be a complete woman at the age of thirty-four. However, when I met Jesus at twenty-two years of age. I experienced a deep spiritual relationship with him and the father. Being born again, changed my life traumatically. It gave me security, a great contentment that transformed me into the women I am today. Jesus' power is so awesome that it revived every dry bone in me. I was able to clearly see my destination. I was able to see my plans he had in my life. I was able to see who my true friends were. I began to hold on to things that were important to me again. I am truly a witness that can say, "His power is made perfect in weakness."

The Lord gave me a high calling to walk in the office as a prophet. He gave me a strict message to give to the churches and the sinners. I said Lord, "I would speak whatever you want me to speak; I would go where ever you want me to go. The people there need an awakening in Israel and the United States and across all the nations." The Lord has put it on my mind that there's some secrecy, some hidden things that are going on unnoticed.

That's why the Lord gave me this message; he gave me a message that will pierce the ears of the listeners. It's a silence that has been long overlooked. It's some people here today that may be a part of this secrecy, and some may be a victim of it. Moreover, the word of the Lord came to me saying: However, it's time to reveal the hidden things. To bring what was done in darkness to the light (amen). We're about to experience some world changes and a very dreadful period of god's wrath.

The opening of the fourth seal of God's judgement. The Lord's [punishment] is at hand to those that are worshipping the beast. The darkness that I am going to expose is the secrecy of the increasing spread of witchcraft thru out the government, churches, and people of all nations. The spirit of antichrist has come into the world, this is evidence that the end is near. According to the book of John, "Even now many antichrists have come. This is how we know it is the last hour. They went out from us, but they did not really belong to us. For if they had belonged to us, they would have remained with us; but their going showed that none of them belonged to us." My conclusion of the matter is to flee Satanism; (The time to receive Jesus Christ should be your only agenda. The world is coming to an end. The Lord's will is not for any of you to perish, he desires that you be caught up in the air to meet him). (The Rapture). (1 Thessalonians Chap. 4 versus 17)

May the Lord Bless you all, Prophetess Sasha Lecher and Evangelist Corinthia Yocheved.

My Messianic Ministry Outreach International web address is www.ikoghmsi.wix.com/ikoghmsi

My 24 hr. prayer request email: ikoghmsi@gmail.com

You may find further info at this site. Facebook: Sasha Lecher, and IKOGHMSI IKOGHMSI.

My office as a prophet will happen sometime during the Fourth and the Fifth seal.

Autobiography

I lived a lie that kept me bound in Satan's chains most of my life. I was a very wretched soul. I found my true spiritual destination through severe loss and much grief.

www.ingramcontent.com/pod-product-compliance
Lightning Source LLC
Chambersburg PA
CBHW052101070526
44584CB00017B/2287